Mosaic of Grace

by James Prescott

Endorsements for *Mosaic of Grace*

"In his well thought-out and delightful book *Mosaic of Grace*, James Prescott masterfully simplifies the sometimes-grandiose theological concept of grace. Through personal narrative and helpful insights, Prescott draws the reader in. His work couldn't be more relevant as we live in a time where we often are defined by our achievements, and the ability to share those achievements through social media. Prescott does an incredible job of reminding us of the simple yet revolutionary notion that in the Kingdom of God, your value is defined by who you are not what you achieve. Thankfully, our identity is and always has been a 'child of the Divine.' For anyone looking to understand grace or be encouraged that they are indeed 'enough,' Prescott's book is a must read!"
Rev. Sarah Heath, author, pastor, and artist
www.revsarahheath.com

"James Prescott's *Mosaic of Grace* is a powerful reminder of the potency and potential of grace to create true beauty out of brokenness, pain, and failure. With clarity and poise, Prescott takes us on a journey towards redemption, reflecting the true heart of God to us with every single page. If you're a person that has ever experienced the hardships of life, then this book is for you. In its pages, you will find hope, healing, and inspiration."
Brandan Robertson, author of *Nomad: A Spirituality for Travelling Light*, www.BrandanRobertson.com

"In *Mosaic of Grace*, James gives readers a chance to see that Grace isn't just something from God to us or something we offer to others. Grace must also be a gift we give ourselves and embrace fully."
Lisa DeLay, host of the *Spark My Muse* podcast
www.SparkMyMuse.com

"*Mosaic of Grace* brings us that sweet sound many have longed for but have never experienced: the amazing grace of God. James Prescott beautifully explores the nature of grace and powerfully demonstrates, through his own story and in the words of Scripture, that if we let grace into our hearts, it may be uncomfortable, it may be messy, but it will also be healing and transformative. *Mosaic of Grace* is an inspirational reminder that, through Christ, brokenness is not the end but the beginning of a grace-filled life of meaning and purpose."
Jennifer McGill, Mouseketeer, singer, worship leader, and author

"In *Mosaic of Grace*, James leads us in reflections on grace. Often talked about but rarely experienced, grace is elusive. But James is a wonderful guide whose writing creates space for us to be open to receive the gift that accepts us, transforms us, and empowers us to extend grace to others."
Nate Pyle, author of *Man Enough*

"I am so thankful for this book. James Prescott has given us a clear and emphatic picture on the unbound love of God, and how it is the one thing that can truly revolutionize our lives. I am more grateful and rooted in the grace of Jesus because of it."
Nish Weiseth, author of *Speak: How Your Story Can Change the World*

"The way James so vulnerably and transparently shares here about the struggles he's experienced leaves readers with a beautiful reminder that there is hope in the hurt and purpose in the pain. Our Heavenly Father is the expert Artist, the only One who can make something truly beautiful out of all the broken pieces of our lives."
Shelly E. Johnson, musician, author of the song, "Mosaic of Grace"

"In an age of polarization and angst, James Prescott leans into his life and the wisdom of Scripture to show us a beautiful picture of the redemptive power of grace. *Mosaic of Grace* is a lovely depiction of a God who is always ready to pick us up when we're broken."
Mike McHargue, author of *Finding God in the Waves*

Mosaic of Grace

Table of Contents

Kintsugi gives us a beautiful word picture for true grace. And in order to understand grace in a way that positively impacts our lives, it's important to understand what grace is *not*.

When grace is properly defined, it gives us a true sense of value, acceptance, completeness, and unconditional love. That kind of grace guides all we do.

How can we talk about grace in a world with cancer, unanswered prayers, and abuse? Grace must be the lens through which we see and interact with our world.

Owning the truth about who we are—the good and the bad—allows us to grow and break through to become who we are meant to be.

Sometimes when we realize a negative truth about ourselves, we respond negatively—condemning and punishing ourselves. We need grace to move beyond condemnation and take responsibility for our actions. Positive, healthy decisions for change lead us to a healthy relationship with God.

In order to let grace transform us, we must let go of misconceptions.

Truth, the lack of misconceptions, leads us to correct thinking, especially under pressure. True grace holds its shape under pressure, helping us to face the tough parts of life in positive, life-giving ways.

Understanding God and understanding Grace are linked together: How we relate to God and how we "do church" is linked to our definition of grace. A healthy relationship with God and a healthy way to do church flows from our proper understanding of grace.

The concepts of Grace and Law work together. They're not opposites—they're interwoven pieces to make a whole. When understanding the meaning of undeserved grace, we're free from legalism and religious nitpicking—which allows us to actually know our loving God.

Grace can be painful and difficult. It's important to face bad habits, addictions, insecurities, and fears—anything that's painful and is holding us back from receiving the full depth of what God has for us.

We can't make grace cheap or forget its cost, because if grace doesn't cost us anything, it's not grace at all. Grace's cost is not simple or easy. When we open ourselves up to grace, we're called to change into positive, forward action with effort, energy, and personal cost.

With Grace, we can go through the worst events—the most difficult, painful situations—and God can use even those horrible times to transform our lives. Grace is, at its core, a transformational healing and restorative circle—helping us come to terms with difficulty, then growing beyond the difficulty into hope where we help others.

We can't just talk about grace. We have to live it out and practice it. This is grace in action: confronting the world we live in with gracious living. Grace is not a theory. It's a response and an action. Grace is God's change agent to us—and to the world.

Introduction
Broken Glass

I stood in front of the mirror for what seemed like an eternity.

First, my clothes disappeared. I was naked before the mirror, exposed and full of shame. Nothing was hidden.

Then the mirror began to crack. One crack at first, then two, then three.

Soon, the mirror was falling apart. Shards of glass formed quicker than I could think, and each shard held part of a reflection of me. It was as if my entire naked self was exposed and broken apart in front of my eyes.

The glass fell to the ground in front of my feet. Big pieces, small pieces. All with sharp edges. A mess on the floor.

No chance of salvation. No hope of restoration. Each broken piece bearing a distorted reflection of me.

I sat on the floor and looked at the shattered shards. My shattered life. How could any good come from the broken, destroyed mess in front of me?

But then, a hand that was bloody and scarred came from above....

Patiently, the hand picked up each sliver of glass. Each time the hand lifted a piece it cut the hand, leaving blood on the edges of the shards and more scars on the fingers and palm. But He kept on picking up the pieces...every little one of them.

Soon, none were left on the floor.

I looked up. There, in front of me, stood my mirror again, restored. I had no idea how, but my image had been put fully back together. But within the image were traces of bloodstains weaving within the glass—a deep, rich colour of red within the whole, seeping through and around the cracks.

It was beautiful.

A beautiful mosaic.

My nakedness had gone. I had on new clothes, and I no longer felt shame. The image looked like me, but then again it didn't. Something was different, but I couldn't put a finger on it. Then I understood. The image was me in the future—someone I was not yet, someone with wisdom and peace twinkling in his eye.

The marks of the shattering—scars of the past—remained in the mirrored image. The mistakes. The hurt. The pain. But the red—the blood—had restored the image to something of beauty, restored the brokenness to wholeness.

Then a light began to shine—not from above or from the side, but from within the mirror. Drawing me in. Showing me a pathway that extended into infinity. A new path.

In this moment, I knew both the truth of my brokenness and the hope of my future.

As the shattering of the glass had not been the end, my brokenness and my pain were not the end.

The hand of the Saviour had made my broken life a beautiful mosaic.

June 12, 2013
James Prescott

Foreword

At twenty-one, I went through an emotional crisis of sorts. I quit my studies for the second time, got help for the depression that was bothering me, and moved ten hours away to live with my parents.

One night, while I was packing to move, a friend came over. As we wrapped glasses in old newspaper, she looked at me and said, "I love you to pieces."

I know people say that all the time, but it made me angry. Really angry.

I stood with a glass in one hand and newspaper in the other, and my soul rebelled against the idea that loving someone to pieces was okay.

I never said anything to my friend about how angry her words made me. About how stupid it was to tell someone that your love was going to ruin them.

Instead, I let her words stay with me. I played with them in my head until I decided that I wanted to be loved to wholeness.

That phrase became my prayer: "God, love me to wholeness."

I was already broken. I didn't need someone loving me to pieces. I needed God to love me to wholeness.

I'd been a Christian since I was four years old, but I didn't comprehend grace until I asked God to love me to wholeness and not to pieces.

At twenty-one, what I didn't realise was that it goes against the nature of God to leave us broken. He is a God that redeems, saves, and restores.

God did not leave me where I started. He did not love me to pieces. Instead, he spoke grace into my broken places.

When I asked God to love me to wholeness, all I wanted was to be glued back together, like a piece of broken china—but God had plans to completely transform me.

That's what grace does.

Grace doesn't let us stay where we are, because grace can see who we can become.

Paul and Timothy wrote in Philippians 1:6 about how confident they were that God will complete the work He has started in us, that God will not stop half-way but will finish.

I take great consolation in that.

The Lord completes broken people like me. God picks up the pieces of my life and shapes them into something whole and perfect, by His grace.

It was during my depression that I first read this quote by Ernest Hemingway: "The world breaks everyone and afterward many are strong at the broken places." As I read that quote, grace broke into the broken places in my life—reminding me that grace isn't for those who say they are fine but for those who believe that life can be different.

As I read *Mosaic of Grace*, I was reminded of these truths once again. The fact that God doesn't leave us broken, that he completes what he has started, and that many times it is in the scars from the broken places that we find who we are and give God permission to use us.

I think that James' message about grace is so effective because he is so honest with his own struggles. He puts in black and white what many of us are scared to whisper in an empty room. After all, isn't that where grace has the most effect? When grace reaches the dark, secret, places where we try to hide from others, real transformation comes.

I love that James has written a book not only about grace but also about becoming who God wants you to be. Grace that doesn't move you towards something better isn't really grace at all. Grace that isn't transformative is simply indulgence.

If you like your life exactly the way it is, I wouldn't read this book. You can't encounter the messy, violent, uncomfortable grace that James writes about and stay the same. But then again, who would want to stay the same when God is offering you an invitation to let His grace love you to wholeness?

Wendy van Eyck

Chapter 1: Myth
Finding Grace

"I believe in a God of scandalous grace.
I have pledged allegiance to a King who
loved evildoers so much he died for them,
teaching us that there is something worth dying for
but nothing worth killing for."
Shane Claiborne[1]

In the late 15th century, a man called Ashikaga Yoshimasa sent a damaged Chinese tea bowl to China to be fixed. It returned, held together with ugly metal staples. This ugly repair launched the Japanese craftsmen on a quest for a new form of mending pottery that could make a broken piece look as good as new—or better.

The process of repair invented was called Kintsugi. Kintsugi is the art of fixing broken ceramic pieces together with a lacquer resin made to look like solid gold. Kintsugi literally means "golden joinery," and often the craftsmen used genuine gold powder in the resin.[2] When the broken pieces are placed back together with the gold resin, an amazing, intricate design is created within the pottery.

In another story, a man took clay pots to his friends in Japan, only for the pots to break en route. He threw the broken pots into a garbage bin, thinking nothing more of the pieces. But when the man departed his friends' home, he was given a gift. Opening the gift, the man found the once-shattered bowls, now put together with Kintsugi—making the pots even more beautiful than their original form.

---

[1] Shane Claiborne, *The Irresistible Revolution* (2006), Zondervan Publishing, p. 315.

[2] More on Kintsugi can be found at the following sites: https://dicklehman.wordpress.com/2013/04/18/kintsugi-gold-repair-of-ceramic-faults-2/ and http://www.thisiscolossal.com/2014/05/kintsugi-the-art-of-broken-pieces/ and http://www.huffingtonpost.com/val-jon-farris/from-broken-to-beautiful-_b_5903994.html and BenzlePorcelain.com, accessed March 11, 16.

Vessels fixed by Kintsugi look more beautiful, more precious, than before the fractures.

In Kintsugi, it is actually in the brokenness that a plate or bowl discovers it's true value—a greater value than would have ever existed before, if it were not broken.

"Being Blessed"

Our culture tells us that it's when we have it all together, when life is good and all our ducks are in a row, then we are blessed. It sells us an ideal story of how we're meant to live without any mess, any brokenness.

The story that western culture sells us goes something like this: You work hard at your job. You get a promotion and a raise in pay. You behave correctly. Then you find a partner and settle down. Finally, you get the blessings from God.

It's a reward-based culture. Our actions define our reward, and once we've dealt with our issues, we can be blessed. Blessing comes after dealing with the mess, not in the midst of it.

We all know this isn't true.

We all know life is messy. And we all know, underneath the surface, we're all broken.

Our Self Concept and Grace

I've believed the lie that says I need to have my life together before I can "be blessed." The lie that says if I am to achieve success or receive the blessings I desire the most, I need to have it all together.

That lie has often made me feel worthless. Useless. Beyond redemption.

Many of us believe the lie that we're not good enough. We think we can't be beautiful if we're broken.

What we fail to see is that, like Kintsugi pots, God uses our brokenness to make us even more beautiful. It's the place of our brokenness where God comes in to restore and renew.

And he does this restoration, this renewal, though grace.

When I uncovered the truth of grace, it was life changing. It was humbling and deeply moving. It opened me to a peace I never thought possible.

I still believe the lie sometimes, because it's easy to slip back into bad habits. But then I'm reminded of the truth. God loves me as I am. Right here. Right now. Today. Even in my mess.

And it's the same for all of us.

"Having it All Together"

Grace is sold to us as some smiley-happy quality only found on perma-grin, overly optimistic Christians who often talk patronizingly about suffering as if it didn't really happen. Grace is sold as an emotion felt at specific moments in our lives—and usually when we have our lives together.

We know the world doesn't work that way.

The strange thing about the myth of *having it all together* is that many of us believe *everyone else* has life in order. *They* are fine. *Those people out there* are doing well. I'm struggling, but *those people* are great.

I've definitely been guilty of this one. But what I've discovered over time is that some of the wisest people I know have also been some of the most broken people.

I'm sure that if I asked you to share honestly whether you believed you had your life together, you'd probably say, *no*. If I asked about some of your acquaintances, people who've met you—not necessarily the ones closest to you, but still those who know you—whether they think you have it all together, probably you'd say, *yes*.

Therein lies the myth: That lives are perfect, that others have everything sorted and in order. And if only we had all they did (or were more like them), then suddenly everything in our lives would be sorted, too.

The truth is, there's no one who has it all together. Not one person.

Every single one of us is like shattered glass. Broken, smashed, and thrown all over the place. With sharp, painful pieces lying strewn and unordered on the floor. And some pieces are so sharp, we would bleed if they were touched.

Insecurities

Have you ever thought, "If I Tweet/say/share what I really think, I'll be exposed and everyone will lose respect for me"?

Me, too.

One night awhile back, I was interacting with some friends online. We had all bought the same online course at the same time. I found out that everyone else had received access to the course a few days prior, yet I hadn't. Normally, it wouldn't be a big deal. But this particular night, the incident snared one of my deepest insecurities:

The fear of being excluded. Left behind.

You see, I've never been part of the "in crowd." At school, this meant being left out and the last to be picked. So in this particular moment with my friends, I felt like the schoolboy once again.

The incident touched a deep past pain. Past pain can have a lot of power over us. If we're not careful, it can control our habits, our behaviour, and how we approach—and respond to—relationships and experiences. In fact, in order to make us fit the not-true view of the past, you and I might punish ourselves through addictions, anger, self-harming, and similar types of behaviour—all of which are rooted in the pain from the past.

This is exactly where I was.

Afterward, at home, I felt low and the night felt very dark. All I wanted to do was let out my frustration, to scream out and to find someone who would listen. I didn't care about manners. I was hurt and wanted answers as to why I—as I perceived it—was "being left behind yet again." Yes. I know. Not a good way to think.

Instead of letting loose in my pain (which would have been a poor choice), I sent a Tweet saying that a few things were difficult for me right then, and I needed prayer.

However, I wasn't as polite with God. He knew the turmoil inside of me, that I felt abandoned by Him. It's still amazing to me how the hurt of the past can so influence the present. I had a good rant at God, and I didn't hold anything back.

Have you ever done that?

Well, it helped. In fact, I believe the Tweeting was God's way to respond to me. Support, prayer, passages from Scripture, and words of encouragement came. Reading these, I experienced a touch of God's grace.

A piece of me was put back together.

Looking back at how I felt that evening, it was totally irrational, childish, and nonsensical. My actions seem ridiculous in the calm light of day. My mature, adult self knows that the rejection that I felt was a bunch of lies. But the insecurities are real. That night, they were part of me. I didn't make them up.

The fear I felt was tangible, and I had to acknowledge it.

The Secret

Here's the point: My healing was made easier only once I remembered the untold secret about insecurities. It's the secret many people know, but no one ever dares to speak out loud.

It's not a secret, really. It's a fact. The fact that we're all like broken pottery.
We all have insecurities. Every. Single. One. Of. Us.
Some are just better at giving the impression to others (and often to themselves) that the insecurities don't exist. We look at everyone else

(those who "have it all together") then look at ourselves—the self no one else sees.

Recently, I posted on Facebook about my insecurities about writing. What happened? Again, responses came. But these responses said that everyone else had the exact same insecurities that I had.

No one has it all together. All those people you admire? The people you consider most wise and great role models? Even them.

At first, I found the truth difficult to accept: those I admire have gaping faults. But once I acknowledged the truth, my own struggles suddenly became easier. Because I realised, if we all have insecurities, then we're all in this together. None of us are really alone.

Grace is not found in *having it all together*, when we have all our ducks lined up and when everything is sorted.

We're united by our brokenness.

Grace in the Pain

Grace is not the great miracle that "makes everything okay," either.

I heard a true story about a member of a church who died. The pastor and some other leaders prayed for the individual, and that person actually rose from the dead. But then, less than a year later, the same pastor lost his wife to cancer. And there was no rising from the dead, this time.

There was no happy-ever-after to the pastor's grief.

So many times, life doesn't turn out okay. A marriage ends. The person you love dies. Grace doesn't suddenly come along and sort it all out. It doesn't lessen the problem, and it doesn't solve it, either. So why talk about grace at all?

That's a great question.

There seems to be so little grace in the world. Many of us don't even know what grace means anymore. The word has been so abused,

James Prescott

misinterpreted, and amalgamated into Christianese.

Grace has to be redefined.

Redefining Grace

Because grace is at the heart of our faith, grace is fundamental to how we see God and how we interact with Him. And the true meaning of grace is so much more than what we think.

Authentic grace allows us to experience deeper intimacy with the Divine.

Grace is finding hope in the mess. It's discovering a hand to cling to when you are in the midst of the darkest hour. It's about acknowledging the shattered glass of life—and piecing it back together.

As any writer will tell you, the best stories aren't the ones where it all works out well. Meaningful stories have conflict, disruption, and struggle—acknowledging the messy world. These stories speak the truth: that life is not simple or easy.

Yet, painful stories in our lives often make us want to run away. To curse God, to ignore Him, blame Him, and retreat into anger, bitterness, and hurt. But running and blaming is the last thing to do, because it's in the moments of pain where we truly discover Divine Grace.

Grace is not about the perfect life we're led to believe we "should have." Grace includes experiencing conflict and suffering. When we feel like giving up, grace strikes us with its hope and love, even in the midst of pain.

Grace is so much more than an emotional feeling. It's not about the smiley-happy face.

It's about discovering the divine in the messiness of our broken lives.

Transformation

Grace is also about transformation. When things get so bad that we feel we don't have any hope left, and when our weaknesses are exposed and we feel like there is no escape, grace faces the pain.

An addiction.
Problems handling finances.
Shameful secrets.
Infidelity.
Poor attitudes.

Behaviours know we need to be free of but want to hold on to. Or a life we want to escape from but feel trapped in.

Grace confronts us with the truth of who we are. It strips us bare and challenges us to change. It tells us we are not condemned, but that we are loved unconditionally, just as we are.

And then, most importantly, grace says we are loved way too much to stay as we are.

Making a Commitment to Change

In the Scriptures, Jesus tells a story about a shepherd who had a hundred sheep but lost one.[3] Instead of looking after the 99, he left to find the one sheep that was lost. Jesus says that this is a reflection of how God loves us.

In the summer of 2013, God took me on a journey into the truth of myself. He showed me the complete train wreck that I am inside and exposed the messiness only He and I know really exists.

On a Sunday that summer, I went forward for prayer at church. I knew I had issues, like all of us, but I felt that I was in control of them. Faced with God's truth, I realized that I was a lost sheep. I had strayed further away from God than I'd thought.

I was suddenly more aware of my state.

---

[3] Luke 15:4-7

James Prescott

The experience of knowing that I had issues to work on overwhelmed me. In that moment, I saw myself with the eyes of the Divine, and I realized how far I had fallen. I recognized how far Jesus had come to find me. I was deeply broken, with all my hurts, anger, failure, and weakness exposed.

As I dealt with the hurt, mistakes, and mess, that I began to hope in who I could become. Knowing the mess that I truly am actually freed me to become all I can be.

Today, I still have struggles and conflicts, of course. I make mistakes. I get humbled. But within the new awareness, I know that the shattered glass of my life is being turned into something more beautiful, as I become the person I'm meant to be.

Embracing Truth

I am a mess. And I am loved.
Inexplicably. Incredibly. Radically.
In my mess.

And so are you.

Yes, even with that habit, that sin, that mistake. You are loved right in the middle of your mess.

Do you know that?

Your life might be as shattered glass. There might be sharp edges that, if you tried touching them, may hurt incredibly. You might be overwhelmed with the dark parts of your life. Or you might feel trapped in a life you don't want to live and a habit you can't seem to break.

But in the middle of it all, you want a transformed life.

Know right now, you're loved and accepted exactly where you are. And grace is waiting to transform.

I have to warn you, though.
Sometimes understanding and embracing God's grace is not a wholly

gentle thing. It grabs us, shocks us, prods us, and compels us. It has an edge. An edge that isn't afraid, if you let it, to make you into the person you were created to be.

Grace-Filled Hope

Grace wants to embrace you, me, and all of us. Grace wants to put us back together again. Not to make everything suddenly okay, but to offer something to hold onto, as we take the first steps out from the place we're in right now.

Do you want hope?

I do.

Hope is possible. Hope comes when we exchange the incorrect way we see the world for the lens of grace.

When our view changes to truth, the shattered glass of our lives is fitted back together into a beautiful mosaic.

A mosaic that doesn't cover the problems we face—but shines the light of Christ onto the problems.

A mosaic that exposes the truth of our lives and compels us to change.

A mosaic that enlightens the problems the world tries to hide and relentlessly transforms them into something positive, good, powerful, and hopeful.

A mosaic that points towards forgiveness, transformation, and a new way of living.

A mosaic that doesn't ignore the past and doesn't cover the pain.

A mosaic that wipes away tears of sadness and turns experiences to joy.

A Kintsugi-like mosaic of grace, more beautiful because of its brokenness, where the scars are marks of transformation.
So let's begin.

Chapter 2: Truth
Grace Defined

---

*"The nuns taught us there are two ways in the world—
the way of nature, and the way of grace.
You have to choose which one you follow."*
Tree of Life[4]

Do you ever feel like you're missing something?

I've often felt like there is something missing from my life. A relationship. A successful career. A bigger pay packet. Or the latest Apple™ product. I try to fill in the missing pieces. But here's the problem: Once one area seems satisfied, I shift my feelings of *missing something* onto another area.

Here's what I mean.

When I had my first serious girlfriend, my desire for a relationship was satisfied. But then I immediately transferred all my angst, frustration, and disappointment for not having a girlfriend to two other areas: my perceived lack of success as a writer and earning a lower salary than many of my peers.

My perceived lack in my life was actually replaced by *two*. (It multiplied.)

This world tells us a lie: that a specific product, relationship, or achievement will satisfy us and fill a hole in our lives. We're fed a story that if we get a great job, find a loving partner and family, and own all the nice material possessions we can get our hands on—and put all our problems behind us—we can be happy-ever-after.

The key word in this story is *lack*.

---

[4] http://www.imdb.com/title/tt0478304/?ref_=nv_sr_1, accessed December 2016.

Where *Lack* Began

Let's go back to the beginning. To a garden. To Adam and Eve.

Satan's words to Adam and Eve were that they lacked something. He said the two lacked the wisdom of God, and that if they ate the fruit from the tree in the Garden, then they would have wisdom. He also told them they could be equal with God if they ate of the apple.

The theology of lack started right there.

This is the first-ever example of good marketing paying off. And, of course, it had disastrous consequences.

But what Adam and Eve (like most of us) didn't realise is that they didn't lack anything—including an intimate relationship with God. They had been created in the very image of God. They needed nothing.

So let's jump forward to today.

In order to restore us to the intimate relationship with God that was broken in the Garden, Jesus died and rose again—the sacrifice of a Son for our broken relationship with God. The whole purpose of the cross and resurrection was to make right what Adam and Eve screwed up.

To reconcile us to our Creator. To set us right with God, once more.

Reconciled with a Gift

In Paul's letter to the Colossians, it says that *through the cross,* Jesus reconciled all things in heaven and on earth to God. The literal translation of the phase, "all things," is (strangely enough) "all things."

Everything reconciled—as in God wanting to bring us back to harmony with him. Getting into a right relationship with God is not just for the people who have it sorted, who fulfil all the commands or rules.

God doesn't love with conditions. Again, the reconciliation—the making right of relationship and the gift of intimacy with our Creator—is for *everyone.* And it's done. "It is finished."

We are all already forgiven, already fully reconciled to God and one with Him, through Jesus. We already have the gift in our hands. We just need to open it. *Opening the gift* is to believe this truth.

Opening the gift it requires us to recognise not just the truth of who God is, but also to recognise how much we need this gift.

Opening the gift means opening ourselves up to the truth most of us already know: That we are broken, messed up, and not living the life we were created to live.

Let's go back to this concept of lack, which caused all the problems in the first place (Adam and Eve). And let's look at how this lack manifests itself in today's world. Because realizing how it plays out today can take us to new understandings.

Grace with You and Me, Today

The culture we live in is fundamentally flawed.

For the last century, our culture has been moving more and more towards a reward-based, entitlement-orientated, self-centred perspective. This perspective has shifted away from a real, truth-filled, Christ-orientated culture.

The myth of lack in our culture, and our desire to fill this lack with money, status, power, possessions, and belief systems, has become fully accepted by the western world. Focusing on our lack—what we don't have—is how we orientate our entire world, from top to bottom.

But the problem is this: The concept of lack brings fear. And fear makes us look out for what's best for ourselves, first.

Inevitably, fear creates cultures of great inequality, with power focused on the few—doing the best for the few, not the many. This is totally contrary to the "loving your neighbour as yourself" way of Jesus.

And didn't Jesus say that *perfect love casts out all fear?*

Fear comes from the false idea of lack. We shy away from people who give us something for nothing, because there is such fear and mistrust in our world. We're encouraged to hide our weaknesses and insecurities (our *lack*) because if we admit it, we're perceived to be failures.

Can you see what fear and lack do to us?

You and I need to see the world through the lens of grace. Not fear. Grace says we do not have to fear.

God's truth says that, whether we succeed or fail, wherever we are in life, we are infinitely loved, blessed, and accepted right where we are, how we are.

Today.

Defining Grace

I've used this word *grace* quite a bit.

Grace comes from the Greek words *charis* (kah-ris) and *chairo* (kah-ee-ro), meaning *to rejoice*.[5] Homer defined *charis* as sweetness or attractiveness.[6] And according to *Strong's Concordance*, the word came to represent favour, goodwill, and loving kindness, especially as granted by a superior to an inferior.

I guess you could call grace a sweet kind of favour that changes your life because, in reality, you don't deserve it.

Here's a list of grace definitions, because the Oxford English Dictionary's definition of *grace*[7] is fascinating:

* A disposition to be generous or helpful

---

[5] Found at http://biblehub.com/greek/5463.htm, accessed March 2016.

[6] Ibid.

[7] Oxford Dictionary of English, https://goo.gl/MImb5N (https://books.google.co.uk/) p. 758, accessed March 2016; and http://www.oxforddictionaries.com/definition/english/grace, accessed December 5, 2015.

* Mercy and clemency
* A favour rendered by a person who didn't need to do so
* A temporary immunity or exemption

So, again, grace is something that is given to us—where we're off the hook for what should have happened but didn't.

Defined by God or by Culture

Grace for a Christian is God's gift of love that we can give to others. It's about love, mercy, and protection given to us without any merit on our part.

The world then asks, *so what's the catch?*

But that's the whole point. There isn't a catch.

Grace is, by definition, a gift. With no conditions. For everyone. The only reason we wouldn't benefit from this gift is if we chose not to receive it. It's like having a birthday present wrapped up and in front of us, but not seeing the gift…or choosing to ignore it.

Our world increasingly chooses to ignore it.

There are various concepts of grace in secular culture. Some people see grace simply as beauty or elegance, a way to describe a peacefulness and serenity. Sometimes *grace* is used to describe beautiful sunsets or aspects of creation.

For those outside the Christian church but interested in spirituality, grace is *an attitude*—as something that centres you. *Meditations* may speak of keeping grace in your heart as you walk through life. Defined by secular culture, grace is *an external force* guiding you through life, peacefully allowing you to leave the past behind, allowing you and me release all the pain and move forward freely.

Sounds kind of familiar, doesn't it? The above definition of *grace* could just as easily be talking about the True God. But there *is* a difference between Christian grace and secular grace. Secular definitions of grace are valid, but they don't give the full picture.

Experiencing Grace

We experience the reality of an abstract concept like grace in our own stories. I asked a few friends some questions about grace—and then asked the same people to write me their stories of grace, in more detail. The stories can be found in the upcoming companion book to *Mosaic of Grace* called *Stories of Grace*.

I posed four questions to my friends:
1. What do you think of, when you hear the word *grace*?
2. What do you think the word *grace* means?
3. How has the idea of *grace* been taught to you?
4. What has been your experience with *grace*?

The first friend's meaning of *grace* came in one word: *elusive*.

The second friend said grace is *something I am expected to give, but not receive— except in an intangible way.* Expected to give, but not receive. Grace here is more abstract.

The third friend defined *grace* as *Jesus Christ, the epitome of grace* and *God's mercy towards us, especially expressed through Christ's death on the cross.* Dianna's understanding of grace is in the person and actions of *Jesus Christ.*

Finally, my fourth friend, Paula, said, *for a long time I had no idea of it's [grace's] meaning…not truly. It's only now that I am older I understand that all of life has been a journey towards growth.*

Growth. That's a powerful word.

Paula also said, *grace is about being thankful for the journey we're on. It's understanding that no matter what happens, good or bad, the result is to enhance growth.* So her understanding of grace as a journey is about the process of *personal growth.*

Very different answers:
Elusive.
Gift.
Jesus Christ.
Personal Growth.

Do any of these words describe how you define *grace*? Does your personal story identify with *elusive, gift, Jesus Christ,* or *personal growth*?

Most of us understand little of grace—especially in the midst of suffering. I get that. On the day my Mum died, I wouldn't have understood grace in the way that Paula talked about, as the cornerstone of *personal growth.* With the benefit of hindsight, however, the concept of a thankful, understanding grace enhancing growth certainly rings true for me.

But the question remains: Why so many different ideas of grace? Does *how* grace has been taught to us matter? It certainly has to. The word *elusive* suggests that not everyone finds the concept of grace easy or that grace is positive.

Grace is multi-faceted, like a Kintsugi mosaic.

Grace and Love

No matter your definition, one word can be considered the cornerstone of grace: *Love.*

People of grace give us the gift of love. Even when who we are and how we act screams that we should be despised, ignored, and rejected—grace *gives love.* Love is a value that cannot be calculated by money, status, or any other measure of the world.

The gift of love is the gift of grace. Because of its relationship to love, grace is something that we cannot live without.

It's important to have a true definition of grace—in order to know, to understand, and to personally experience grace. A true definition of grace changes our lives.

James Prescott

Chapter 3: Perspective
What Do Others Say About Grace?

"Grace is everywhere, like lenses that go unnoticed
because you are looking through them."
Phillip Yancey[8]

In my experience, grace is rarely a topic discussed. I think I've heard one sermon in my entire life devoted to grace alone. I can't help thinking, *this isn't right*.

Most of us agree: The world we live in is broken. Messed up. We get happy-clappy Christians talking about grace as magic dust that will make all things okay. That no matter what happens, it's all going to be sorted out in the end. And we should all put perma-grins on, even when we're in the darkest depths of despair.

Such a view of grace can be as damaging as not discussing grace at all.

We all know that things don't always work out the way we want them to. We don't always get the happy-ever-after story that consumerism and Hollywood try to sell us. The all-for-certain happy ending that some Christians talk about never shows up.

Some Christians say you *have* to be healed, and if you don't get healed there's some reason for it—like "unresolved sin" (because, of course, only *specific* people have unresolved sin…insert an ironic voice here). Or there's the argument that if you're not healed or the situation isn't fixed, then God is punishing you for something.

And then there's the idea that God is somehow trying to teach us something, and this horrid tragedy will somehow all work out for good in the end.

Try telling a woman who is being abused that it will all work out for good. Try telling a husband who's losing his wife to cancer, leaving him to bring

---

8 *What's So Amazing About Grace?* (2003), Zondervan, Chapter 3.

up three small children alone, that they have unresolved sin or that God somehow has a plan.

It doesn't make sense.

The fact is, we all suffer.

Children die in infancy.
Family members get cancer.
Women, children, and men are abused.

Problems don't get solved. The loved one isn't raised from the dead. The wife with cancer doesn't always get healed. The abuse doesn't end. And even as people are liberated, more are taken into slavery.

How can we dare speak of grace in a world like this?

If you try to tell someone in the depths of despair about grace—especially if you're a Christian with a perma-grin—then you might get slammed in the face. If someone came to me the day my Mum died and told me it was all going to be okay…or that I had unresolved sin, or that God was punishing me, or that God had a good plan for this…my response would not have been positive.

Because grief and pain are real.

But.
Listen.
(Please.)
It is *precisely because* we live in a world of such grief, pain, suffering, and injustice that *we need grace in the first place*.

We need people carrying grace who meet us in the depths of despair.

In the moments when we're vulnerable, when our weaknesses are exposed, we need grace in love that allows us to grieve and to feel. God's grace simply tells us that no matter how angry, bitter, and depressed we feel—with questions about how nonsensical it all is—we are still accepted. We are still loved.
That is grace.

When people love us even while we don't feel like loving them. That's grace.

When people don't ask anything of us, except that we are who we are at that particular moment. That's grace.

Grace isn't really what others say. It's what people do.

Famous People of Grace

Mother Theresa of Calcutta is often described as a woman full of grace—someone with qualities that are often unexplainable to us, qualities that carry the mark of the Divine.

We all know the way the world works. Often times, it's the most intelligent, most gifted, good-looking, healthy people who "win." The "beautiful people" get the great job and amazing career, to be husband and wife and have wonderful children. With the status, wealth, the great house, great car. And everything falls into place for them, right?

(It's the world's view.)

The people who work the hardest, who are the most talented, get the furthest. It's even like this in many Christian circles—the ones who end up leading, preaching, and "getting all the blessings from God" are the "famous people."

But grace is not only for specific famous people. Or specific types of Christians. Grace is for everyone. No matter what the world says.

There's another view. It's the karma, eye-for-an-eye view of the world. This view says we get what we deserve and that what you do eventually comes back to haunt you. That you'll be punished for everything you've done wrong. We call it *justice*.

But grace is different.

Grace says we are all equally valued—precious children of our Creator God. Grace says we are chosen, and no one is exempt. Even if you've failed at everything you've tried your hand at, you are still loved, accepted, and valued at the end of it all.

Grace says your value, worth, and identity doesn't come from what you do but from *who you are*: a child of the Divine.

Grace says, whatever you've done, whatever your past, whatever your story, whatever your gift, there's a place for you. You're loved and accepted unconditionally. Where you are. Right in that moment.

Bono talks about this scandalous claim of grace like this:

"Along comes this idea called Grace to upend all that 'as you reap, so you will sow' stuff. Grace defies reason and logic. Love interrupts, if you like, the consequences of your actions, which in my case is very good news indeed, because I've done a lot of stupid stuff."[9]

Again, grace is for everyone. It's for those who our culture calls somebodies, like Mother Theresa and Bono, and the ones it calls nobodies, like most of us.

Grace is for all. Equally. Unconditionally.

You see grace isn't just an optional extra for our lives. It's not merely a positive quality to be aspired to and it doesn't apply to only specific types of people. Grace is at the centre of how we're meant to live. Grace is at the core of what it means to be a follower of Jesus. Grace is also intertwined in all we do and who we are.

Grace is entwined with how we view God.
Grace is foundational to how we do church.
Grace is key to our forgiveness.
Grace is wrapped in how we deal with our mistakes—
and the mistakes of those around us.
Grace is at the centre of healing.
And, quite importantly, it's at the heart of how we experience relationships—with others, and with God.

---

[9] *Bono, in Conversation with Michka Assayas* (2006) Berkley Publishing Group, the Penguin Group: London.

The Lens of Grace

When photographers take pictures, the lens they use is critical. There are different lenses: macro or close-up lenses, zoom lenses, specialty lenses. Each lens produces a different photo, even if the shot is taken from precisely the same spot. Camera lenses, used in the wrong context (such as a macro lens for a long-distance shot) won't produce the best picture. The type of lens you use can change everything.

The truth is, we all have a lens to which we view life.

C.S Lewis said, "I believe in Christianity as I believe the sun has risen: Not only because I see it, but because by it I see everything else."[10] Lewis' lens filtered through creation. In this quote, Lewis could have been speaking of grace.

Grace is at the heart of the Christian faith.

The cross is about grace.
How we see others is rooted in how we understand grace.
The heart of discipleship and transformation is a response to grace.
Learning how to forgive is about showing grace.
Pursuing social justice and the values of Jesus in the world is directly linked to grace.
Where we gain our value, worth is rooted in how we receive grace.
Our core identity is grounded in grace.
And our relationship with God is highly impacted by our understanding of grace.

Grace is central to how we live. It's not just a topic of discussion or something on the side that we can choose to pick up or not.

Each of us orients our lives around one story or another. Whatever we believe, that belief originates with set of values—the ways that we deem to be the best way to live. And each of us has a specific way in which we

---

[10] C.S. Lewis, "Is Theology Poetry?" (1945), http://www.samizdat.qc.ca/arts/lit/Theology=Poetry_CSL.pdf, accessed September 5, 2016.

see the world: the lens through which everything and everyone else is filtered.

As the quote at the beginning of the chapter from Terence Malik's "Tree of Life" film so insightfully states, there are essentially two ways in the world: the way of nature and the way of grace. We choose which one we live by.

> The nuns taught us there were two ways through life. The way of nature, and the way of grace. You have to choose which one you follow. Grace doesn't try to please itself. Accepts being slighted, forgotten, disliked. Accepts insults and injuries. Nature only wants to please itself. Gets others to please it over them. To have its own way.... The nuns taught us that no one who loves the way of grace, ever comes to a bad end.[11]

There's so much truth in that quote, isn't there? I mean, when you look at the world we live in, so much of it is simply the way of nature. You might even call it human nature. Secular culture is always advocating the me first philosophy, which is about taking care of ourselves first, before worrying about others.

And just look at how that's turned out. War. Inequality. Abuse. Violence. Poverty. Slavery. The way of nature, the way of self, has proven itself fundamentally flawed.

Perhaps it's time we looked at ourselves, at others, and the world a different way.

What would it be like if we actually did turn the other cheek? What if we didn't hold our identity in what others think of us—or didn't put our value in what we do and what we achieve?

The way of grace is this: Finding our value in the fact we are uniquely created children of the divine, loved and accepted unconditionally as we are, even in the messiness of our lives.

I say it's time for the way of grace. Time to take a step back from the

---

[11] You can find the film on IMDb at http://www.imdb.com/title/tt0478304/.

James Prescott

world, from ourselves, from everything, and refocus—in the context of grace.

I have found that the people I meet who are the most loving, understanding, and forgiving—whether Christian or not—are those who have had true, authentic experiences of grace. Because grace in action transforms our lives and the lives of those around us.

And once we've experienced true grace, we never want to let go of it.

I know that my own experiences of grace have transformed me. With grace, I find it easier to forgive. With grace, I'm less quick to judge and condemn. And with grace, I feel a genuine, deeper concern for others. I don't claim to be perfect, of course, but I am certain that my experience of grace has allowed me to share more of God's grace with others. It has given me the lens that allows me to see others—and God—in a different light.

When we experience grace, it transforms us. It shapes us. And it overflows from us into the lives of others. Grace strips our preconceptions of the world, right down to the bare bones, giving a different perspective on the world and the people we encounter. It tells us a new story—that we lack nothing and we are loved, accepted, and valuable, right now. Even in the midst of our brokenness.

James Prescott

Chapter 4: Own
Grace and Personal Change

———————

"Guilt says, if only you had done it better. Shame says, if only you had been better.
After too many years of this, I admitted it. I am so dysfunctional,
I can't even figure out how to become functional. And, it is alright."
Gerald May[12]

A while back, I went on holiday with some good friends to the southern
European island of Malta. The island is small enough that most places are
within about two hours of travelling time, so we decided to travel by bus
for most of the holiday.

One day on the way back from one of our trips, I stepped off the bus and
promptly tripped and fell forward onto the concrete. Only the instinctive
movement of my hands in front of me stopped my face from hitting the
ground.

Now I have to fess up here.

Truth is, I've always been slightly clumsy. My hand-eye coordination and
sense of balance aren't the best in the world. My clumsiness has kind of
annoyed me and been the cause of several jokes at my expense.

A day or two later on the holiday, it happened again. I was sitting next to
my friends on the deck of an open-air tourist bus. The road was bumpy,
and as we were getting thrown about a bit, my propensity for having
accidents somehow came up in our conversation.

To be frank, I thought they were making way too much of a deal of my
clumsiness, and I argued this point vehemently. Okay, I have a few
accidents occasionally, but I'm not that bad—at least not as bad as some
people.

At the exact same moment, the bus ran over a bump in the road and I was

———————

[12] Gerald May, *The Awakened Heart*, 1993 (Harper Collins), p. 6.

thrown sideways onto the floor. Every single one of us burst into laughter—me, most of all. I laughed so hard I almost lost my breath.

And at this point, I stopped arguing. I just laughed and accepted the truth.

I'm a little clumsy. There it is. And although I can make an effort to avoid these types of incidents, I'm probably going to have the occasional accident.

And it's okay, because it's a part of who I am. So instead of getting upset by it, I can just own it. I can make fun of myself. I can even use it for my own benefit.

Grace is just like this.

Grace rescues us from the truth of who we are. Grace is about me accepting myself as I am, rather than trying to be something I'm not. Maybe clumsiness is not a major issue (and let's face it, it *is* funny, when you think about it). But the principle is the same. I don't have to pretend that I'm not clumsy—or prove myself as poised—in order to be accepted.

Grace is about owning the truth of who we are. Both the good and the bad.

Accepting Ourselves

Grace is accepting the reality of our character, identity, and habits—the *truth*—and then dealing with the consequences of the truth.

In the case of my clumsiness, this means taking a bit more care when I'm walking around and watching where I'm going. Instead of denying the truth and carrying on with the tripping up and falling over, I can do something positive to ensure that it happens less.

But only by owning the truth about myself can I make this change.

Here's another, more serious example from my childhood. When I was very young, my Dad kept a tin of money by his bed. I never knew what this money was for, but it was a lot of money. More than I had ever seen in my life at that point, and most definitely more than I had.

One day, a video of a film came out that I really wanted to buy (there were no Blu-Rays or DVDs back then). I couldn't quite afford the video on my paper round salary. I was so desperate to buy this video that I crept into my Dad's bedroom and took some money from the tin. Not much, but a little. Not enough that anyone would notice.

Or so I thought.

Taking money from the tin became a bad habit of mine. Anytime I saw something I wanted and didn't have the money to get it, I'd creep in my parents' room and steal it.

And that's what it was. Stealing.

Even now, over 20 years later, I still feel the shame when writing these words.

But the thing was, the more I stole from the money tin, the more obvious it became. Until one day, when I stole a £50 note and my Dad was ready. Before I'd even put it away, he came into my room and asked me where I'd gotten the money.

I gave a lame excuse, like it was from my savings. But we both knew the truth.

I was exposed. I was shown for who I was. There was no way to hide. I had no choice but to own the truth of what I had done and take responsibility for it.

He took the money back. I got a telling off, and rightly so. And I never, ever stole again.

It only took me this once to be confronted with the truth. Once I owned my shadow and accepted it—that I'd been stealing and it was wrong—I was able to change.

Now, I had known the truth all along, that what I was doing was wrong. But it was hidden, covered under shadow, not exposed—disguised by the goody-two-shoes image I projected to the world. And I'd been good at projecting this image. Pretty much everyone bought it. Only my father knew about the shadow side.

Today, I have little habits that I'm ashamed of, too. Not stealing (thankfully) or anything illegal. Nevertheless, they're habits I'm ashamed of. And if we're honest, we all have these types of habits—bad habits, no matter how small, that we wish we could get rid of.

Maybe it's an issue in our lives that we brush under the carpet instead of confronting it (like taking money from the tin). Over time, what began as something small can become massive. Because the greater the problem, the more we have to lose by disclosing the issue. The more we're afraid of the consequences.

It's a downward spiral. And the only way out is to *confront what is in the shadows.*

Maybe it's an addiction. Maybe it's a rift between you and someone close—or an act of deceit towards someone you love. Or maybe it's an annoying habit that people around you would rather not see, but they tolerate it because of friendship. And you know, deep down, you need to deal with it.

The longer we leave the issue hidden, the more difficult it becomes. The truth is, the only way to be transformed and move forward is by owning our shadow.

Of course, it's challenging.

We know that by owning our shadow, there will be consequences. If we have a habit, we're going to have to admit it to those we love—which will most likely be painful. We may realise just how much the issue negatively impacted others, and we'll be quite down on ourselves, no doubt.

That *fear of consequences* is what's keeping you and me from changing. But this is where grace comes in.

We Think Grace will Hurt, But Grace Heals

Grace is counter-intuitive. We think that admitting the issue will destroy us. But it, in fact, admitting issues heal us.

Grace strikes us in these moments of admission. When we admit the darkness in our lives, instead of shame and fear, we find love, healing, and acceptance. Where there is true grace, fear and shame pass away. It's only when we own the truth about ourselves that we can then begin the journey of healing and transformation.

Alcoholics Anonymous is an organisation teaching us much about grace. What's the first step people who attend need to take? That's right. Confess the person is an alcoholic. And for someone who has most likely denied this truth for a long time, owning up to the truth can be difficult. But once an alcoholic finally admits the truth (to themselves *and* in front of others), transformation and healing begins.

However, sometimes we aren't aware of our inner shadows that can turn into monsters. We all have blind sides. It occasionally takes others—and God Himself—to point out the issues.

We can get a glimpse of our inner shadows when we actually take the time to stop and think on what we've said or done. Being self-aware. Or we can get it through the convicting word of a friend. Being open to others. Or it can even come when we sense God speaking to us directly, during prayer. Being open to God.

Looking back at the ways I've spoken or acted towards people, even in recent times, I see the shadows in my life and the monster I can be. In those moments, I almost feel like I want to curl up and die.

Here's one major example.

I had a friend years ago…someone who (like me) liked to be right all the time. And who was intelligent enough to articulate a good argument. This person used to wind me up something chronic. In friendly banter and in jest, he argued with me, pointed out weaknesses, and in general gave me a hard time—*all the time*. What was said was meant in good fun—never in malice—but it hurt. My friend's banter irked me because I knew that some of the assumptions he made about me weren't true. Inside, I wanted to shout and explain that he didn't know what he was talking about. Did you ever feel this misunderstood? I think we all do. So what did I do?

I became embittered towards this person. Angry. I began to feel jealous because in comparison to my life, his life was a bed of roses. I had gone through my parents' divorce, then losing a parent, and for him, everything seemed to turn out just fine. *Life just wasn't fair,* I thought.

The friend moved away, and we don't see each other as often as we used to. Our distance and growing maturity has given me a healthier perspective. (Hang with me here. There's a point to this story, and it's coming.)

All this time, I'd made myself the victim in the relationship. I'd assumed that I wasn't at fault in our communication issue. According to me, I wasn't to blame. But over time, apart from each other, as I reflected and saw our relationship more objectively, I realised I had been as much to blame as the other.

We had a great misunderstanding.

The other person wasn't really being cruel. He thought he was being funny. Sometimes, he was trying to help me. I had to admit, with my sometimes over-sensitivity, I'd turned the feelings into something like bullying. But he wasn't He was pointing out of my flaws in with a desire for me to learn and grow, not out of a desire to make me look bad. And maybe, just maybe, I might have been winding him up, too. Ahem.

In reflection, I saw that I was unable to get his message or to take note of his advice. And my arrogance showed: I assumed that I had nothing to learn. Which probably hurt him, as well. It was a two-way street.

I was faced with the truth that I had hurt him as much as he had hurt me. As I realised this, I began get that feeling inside—the one you get when you realise you've screwed up. You know the feeling I'm talking about? It's the feeling right down in the depth of your heart, deep inside. The painful feeling making you want to reach inside, find the offensive part, and simply rip it out—just so you don't have to feel that way anymore.

I couldn't shake it. Because I knew it was the truth. How was I going to mend this?

In the process of grace, I had to spend time examining myself. Reflecting on my mistake. And being open to how I could learn from it. There was no way I could do that on my own. I needed to go deeper. I needed to deal with it on a spiritual level.

If I didn't go deeper, I would be glossing over the issue. You can deal on an intellectual, psychological, and emotional level. And all those things are helpful. But none of these are sufficient alone. There's a level beyond that, where the issue only makes sense when you bring God into the picture.

The Deeper Grace with God

I had to go back to God and repent, to ask forgiveness, and to ask Him to help me live differently, with a different attitude. To realise I'm not always the victim, and sometimes I'm as guilty as those I assume are out to hurt me.

I've since met other friends who like to wind me up and make jokes; they also say words that I don't want to hear. Previously, I would have become embittered towards these people. But instead of being arrogant and getting bitter, I've come to understand my sensitivities. I've realised their type of humour is because they care. And even if I don't agree, I need to at least consider them.

My relationship with my old friend has been completely transformed. I get on with him now better than ever. And the change came through me.

Through owning my own shadow, I have been able to receive forgiveness. I have been able to experience grace. And this has allowed me to be transformed.

It's only when we own our shadow that we can receive forgiveness and grace.

If we continue with a way of life outside of God's plan for us, letting sin dictate to us how we respond to life, then how can we possibly receive forgiveness from God and others?

Grace isn't something we get if we *do something*. Grace is a gift we can *receive*…if we are honest with ourselves.

Grace saves us from the truth of who we are by allowing us to begin the process of change.

In the Bible, in the book of John, is a story of a woman who Jesus met at a well. At the beginning of her interaction with Jesus, she tried to hide her past. But her actions—going to collect water at lunchtime, when no one else in the village would be there—gave her away.

Of course, Jesus knew the truth. In love, He proceeded to name the truth in her life. He spoke about her many husbands of the past and her current partner who wasn't her husband. When He spoke the truth, she didn't even attempt to conceal it.

What's important here is that instead of judgment, this woman found an invitation to move in a new direction with her life. Being called out was an opportunity to drink a new type of water from a different kind of well. She found a Saviour who loved her—even when He knew the truth about her.

And with facing the truth of her life, she was transformed by the Saviour's love.

She actually became an evangelist for Jesus, preaching His message to her whole village. She was a whole different person. She saw a life beyond—and was no longer defined by her past.

Owning the truth set her free. It allowed her to receive grace, embrace forgiveness, and be liberated to a life she never imagined.

Owning the Shadow

If we can't own our own shadow, we can't be transformed. And we can't become the person Jesus created us to be—which, by the way, might be a whole lot more than we'd first imagined.

Grace so often gets tied up with some smiley, happy, emotion where everyone feels good and gets off scot-free, with hippie-style peace and love. And whilst peace and love are a part of grace, they aren't the whole story. If we are to truly experience grace, we are not going to feel great all the time.

True grace can be violent. It takes hold of us and strips us down. It can make us feel like we want to rip our hearts out. It exposes us for the world to see. And it compels us to change. It leaves us no option but to be transformed.

It's when we embrace our darkness—when we allow grace to tear us apart, to shatter the mirror of our lives—that we can receive healing and transformation.

When people speak of grace, especially religious people, they often want to avoid the crucifixion and jump straight to the resurrection. The attitude of everything being a celebration, without understanding and recognising the reality of suffering, seems to be a part of the church more and more. But we must understand grace, because any misunderstanding about the *pain of grace* impacts people's ability to experience *true grace*.

By ignoring the crucifixion, we choose to avoid conflict, pain, struggle, and the exposure of our weaknesses. To just move on to the good feeling of resurrection actually hurts us. Grace that ignores Friday and heads straight to Sunday, in truth, isn't grace at all.

We all have our own pain and death to deal with. And resurrection only happens after death.

I could have kept ignoring my poor attitude to my relationships with others. I could have kept on being arrogant and thinking I had all the answers, letting myself get wound up and angry—playing the victim, becoming embittered.

The only way for me to move forward was to admit the truth, facing up to the reality of my bad attitudes—and then choosing to live differently.

Facing the truth, for me, was painful. It was difficult. But once I walked through the valley of that pain, I was able to take positive steps forward to grow more into the type of man I want to be. To be the man that God created me to be.
It was a decision. And a process.

As I went through the process of allowing grace to do its work, I experienced a depth of love and acceptance in my spiritual life I had never felt before. On the realisation of the process working in and through my life, I was moved to tears more than once. And in the process, I felt an intimacy with God that I had never felt before.

Grace had torn me apart. But it had resurrected me, because I had not been afraid to own my own shadow.

The lesson I learned above all was this:

Learning the way of grace is about truth. It's reconciling the truth, of both our own infinite value and of others' infinite value—despite our depths of brokenness.

Chapter 5: Us
Grace with Ourselves

"How we fall into grace. You can't work or earn your way into it.
You just fall.
It lies below, it lies beyond. It comes to you, unbidden."
Rick Bass[13]

I went through a really dark time in the decade after my mum's death. It was a time of counselling, prayer, and healing. There was lot of focusing on me by looking inwards. And whilst this was healthy, there was always a danger that I could begin to think that life was all about me.

When focusing on myself, I could forget to focus on others.

Well, it happened. I began to play the role of the victim. I'd been bullied my entire teenage years. I grew up in a broken home where I frequently stepped in to stop fights between my parents. So losing my mum just added to the sense of feeling that life was against me.

Rather, that God was against me.

This sense of rejection from God sank deep into my soul, beyond my conscious self. For a long time, the feelings of despair became my identity. I turned every conversation onto myself. I became a good pity party host.

In the meantime, I began to lose friends. And I felt that losing those friends was about *them*. I'm not the most sociable, outgoing person. I'm an introvert. I'd always been outside cliques my entire life, so this was nothing new. I made assumptions that people who'd stopped talking to me had decided they didn't want to be friends with me because I didn't "fit" with them.

In my mind, it was never about me. I thought I was a good person. I cared about others and tried to do what was best for them. Certainly, my intention was always to serve. I wanted to bless, support, and encourage

---

[13] Rick Bass, *Colter, (2000)* Houghton Mifflin, p. v3 (prologue).

others. There was never any malice in my behaviour, and I honestly didn't believe I was being selfish.

But one summer, my thinking changed.

The Starting Point of Fully Trusting God

I was in the pub with a friend and we were talking about trusting God. I shared how that, because of my past, I struggled to trust anyone, let alone God. How I'd never let God into my heart fully because I was too afraid. My past had made me a control freak. I didn't want to trust anyone fully because I was afraid of being hurt, and I was afraid of the unknown.

Through our transparent conversation, my friend challenged me (and eventually convinced me) that my attitude had to change. I knew my friend was right, that I had to let God in, to break down the wall around my heart—whatever the consequences may be.

So my friend prayed with me. Right there, in the pub. We prayed I would let God into my heart, and I gave God permission to break down the wall of self-protection and come into the places that I'd left Him out of. I needed to let God infiltrate those areas that I'd kept from him.

I didn't know it then, but this moment would transform my life.

Transformed to Change

For the next month, I felt like God's love, grace, and peace filled me up to the brim. I kept getting encouraging words from others about my gifts, my calling—and words from God about my own value and worth. I began to see how much I was loved by God.

It felt good.

But the month afterward, I started to hear a different message. The tone of what God was doing changed.

Over the second month, God showed me other truths about myself. Truths I didn't want to hear. Truths about my character, my bad habits, and how my actions had hurt others and separated me from God.

One day, I was walking home from church with friends. For a reason I don't remember, I began to act like the victim again, getting down on myself, moaning again about this, that, or the other thing. But this time, my friends didn't let it go. They didn't just ignore or brush my actions aside. They called me on it.

They told me I played the role of the victim all the time, how it was impacting others, and how I needed to get out of that role. How I fished for compliments—subtly, but obviously, too. How I talked about myself too much.

It wasn't good to hear. I knew deep in my gut they were absolutely spot on.

That day (and for some time after, as I reflected on my friends' words), I realised just how selfish I'd become and how my actions had hurt others. I'd gone way too far and made being a self-obsessed victim a way of life.

Then a light came on.

I understood: The reason some people had stopped speaking to me wasn't because they were bad people (as I'd suspected). It wasn't that I'd been left out deliberately because I wasn't part of the "clique."

No. My own behaviour, actions, selfishness, and pity seeking had pushed people away.

I was so self-involved that people became tired of me. I didn't blame them, because all I did was take. I was inward looking, and not loving or generous.

It was a realisation that I had poor character, and I was ashamed. Even horrified. When I looked at other men my age—the men with good character I respected, admired, wanted to be like—and I examined myself in comparison, I saw a pale reflection of those men.

I hadn't intended to be this way. But that's who I'd become.
Have you ever felt this way?

Taking on the Truth

There was no one else to blame but me. I was more than humbled. I felt like I'd been stripped bare before the entire world. Humiliated. And the pain was intense.

I broke down and wept. I had no excuses, no justification for my actions.

I was confronted by the stark reality of my own brokenness, my own need for forgiveness and grace. I realised it was way too late to go and ask everyone for forgiveness.

I was in a place to receive grace.

But that's not what happened.

Grace for Ourselves

Instead of receiving God's grace, I began to punish myself. Instead of taking a healthy responsibility for my actions, I began to wallow in self-pity, saying how worthless, useless, and horrible I was. I told God I didn't deserve anything from Him.

It's often easier to push away or even punish ourselves, rather than accept that we're loved, despite our mistakes. (Come on. You've done this before too, right?)

I became depressed. Instead of being transformed, I felt worthless, useless. That's what happens when you punish yourself. I had no grace with myself.

You see, when we are confronted with ourselves—when God shows us who we really are—then it's easy to punish ourselves. We feel we don't deserve blessing, we don't deserve to be loved as God loves us, and we don't deserve forgiveness or grace.

Instead of responding positively to the truth of who we are, we may sink into a pit of despair. Despair is as bad, if not worse, as not being convicted of sin in the first place. It doesn't change us for the better. It makes things worse.

Without hope, we're overwhelmed and our lives will get worse, not better. Overwhelm comes because we haven't walked through resolving the issue with God. And if we don't walk through it with God, we can become paralysed by our brokenness.

So we must not walk through pain alone. We must walk our soul's shadows with Jesus. Accepting grace from God, we must also show grace to ourselves.

Does this mean that we smile and say that it's all okay?
Of course, not.

The Healthy Place Between

A healthy response to having our lives stripped bare before God is neither to dwell in darkness nor pretend there's nothing wrong.

Yet, it is often in one of these two places that Christians tend to live.

Christians in this situation often act either like there is no problem at all or cover up the problems—even though we're fully aware of the problems deep down. Or we act negatively, saying we're lowly worms, worthless and not deserving good from God.

The church does this, too.

How many churches are run by fear? They speak a message of how worthless and useless we are in comparison to God. Or they say that unless we say yes to God, we will burn for eternity.

None of these approaches is loving or full of grace. The approach that reflects grace is, in its truest sense, somewhere in-between.

Taking Responsibility

Accepting grace is acknowledging and taking responsibility for our darkness.

It's about knowing we're not perfect. It's accepting that we're in need of forgiveness, healing, and grace. Yet, at once, it is knowing at our core that we're infinitely and unconditionally loved. There is forgiveness, healing, and grace on offer to us.

Each and every time, there is a new life, a new beginning to be had. We live in the knowing that restoration, reconciliation, and rebirth are possible at any moment, no matter how low we may have sunk.

I was talking to a close friend about how I often punish myself, and he said, "You'd never treat your friends the way you treat yourself." The same is true of divine grace. God doesn't want us to punish ourselves—He wants us to have grace with ourselves. We need to have the same grace with ourselves that God has with us.

The Scandal of Grace

When we don't have grace with ourselves, we deny both our divine identity and worth and put ourselves out of God's reach. Not having grace with ourselves could even be called a sin. If we don't have grace with ourselves, then we deny the healing and restorative powers of the divine.

We are saying that God's love isn't *enough*. That His grace doesn't extend to us, and it never will.

Punishing ourselves for our sin (instead of taking responsibility for it) and saying we're not deserving of God's love, grace, and forgiveness, *rejects* grace instead of receiving it. In reality, we're judging ourselves, when only one person is meant to judge us: God.

So often, we condemn people for being judgmental of others, whilst forgetting we can be judgmental of ourselves. It's just as bad to judge and condemn our own self as it is to condemn others.

God's complete love and acceptance of us is a scandal of grace.

When we see ourselves as God sees us, we're convicted. We see how broken we are, and the natural human reaction is to want to judge and punish ourselves. We want to decide for ourselves the punishment we deserve, and then inflict this punishment on ourselves.

Even worse, if we adopt the self-punishing attitude, it impacts how we treat others: when we're unforgiving of ourselves, we find it increasingly difficult to love and forgive others.

In other words, if we don't have grace with ourselves, we end up judging others.

Judgment creates more pain, suffering, and disconnection from God. Judging others often results in people rejecting God and leaving the church. Judging also further emphasises the image of God as a dictator who is interested only in condemning us and sending us to hell at a moment's notice. It's the view of a "getcha-God" who waits for us to screw up. It's a distant God who isn't interested in love or mercy but only in condemnation.

A God without grace.

But this view is completely upside down.

In order to fully receive the grace of God and for the world to reflect God's heart of love, grace, justice, and mercy—the world God intends— we must first have grace with ourselves.

It begins with you and me.

Forgiving ourselves is to remember the truth that no matter what we have done, we are infinitely loved. And the love and grace of God is sufficient—no matter how low we've gone.

Despite the amount of pain we cause others, how selfish we can be, how rude and unloving we can act, God still forgives us. He still loves us exactly the same. And His grace is enough, for you and for me.

Our View of God

How do you see God? Do you see Him as a judgmental tormentor out to get us or as a loving Father wanting the best for us?

He wants us to face the truth of who we are. But He is not waiting to condemn or hurt us, when we see the truth. He waits to forgive us, to shower us with grace—and to help us live a transformed life. He's not a God of terror. He's a God of grace.

For me, as I dealt with the truth of my behaviour and received God's grace, I was overwhelmed by love and forgiveness and I began to weep tears of joy. I had no response but to say *thank you* as the warmth of God's love and grace washed over me.

As I dealt with behavior and showed myself more grace, I felt an almost instinctive, natural desire growing within me to live a different life. To choose to live in the way God created for me.

There is a realistic, authentic hope that you and I can be better. The only reasonable response, then, to this kind of God-Grace is sheer thankfulness and authentic transformation that brings us to a deeper love for God than you and I have ever had before.

Now I don't want to give the impression that I've got it all sorted. I still struggle with not punishing myself and with forgiving others. That's human. But through having grace with myself, I'm learning to let go of anger, bitterness, and hurt.

Grace allows me to feel more liberated, to love other people more fully.

That's such a better way to live.

James Prescott

Chapter 6: God
What's the Truth About Grace?

———————

*"The grace of God means something like: Here is your life.
You might never have been, but you are because
the party wouldn't have been complete without you."*
Frederick Buechner[14]

I was taken to church from a young age, so I began my Christian journey almost from birth. While growing up, my view of God was that He was only a distant divine being. Yes, he was loving, caring, and just. But He was far away, and I was a "sinner." I had screwed up really badly, and if I didn't follow the correct religious rules and procedures, I was headed to hell.

It was that simple. And not surprisingly, I was a bit scared of God. But I thought the fear was fine as it was the "fear of the Lord," which is, according to Proverbs, the beginning of wisdom.

Or so I was told.

How I Viewed God and Grace

I prayed a lot growing up—but to Jesus, not to God. In hindsight, I prayed that way because I was terrified of God Himself. I made sure I kept all the religious rules and did all the right things—but only because I was terrified of what would happen if I didn't. When I messed up, I said sorry and tried to live differently, asking for forgiveness. But it felt like I was a schoolboy going to the headmaster's office with my head bowed in fear and shame, not as a child going to His loving Father.

With this perspective, I struggled with inner change. Deep down, I never felt comfortable with the far-away God who brought feelings of fear. It made me feel like I had to do something to get on God's good side. I wasn't mature enough, wise enough, or Christian enough to receive those

———————

[14] http://www.frederickbuechner.com/content/grace-god, accessed December 4, 2015.

things called "blessings." Maybe I was missing something.

Grace wasn't even on the agenda.

Not a very healthy view of God, is it?

Even through my university years, as I matured in faith and grew in my relationship with God, there was still an underlying feeling that God wasn't intimate. And grace wasn't something I really thought about.

The Seeds of Change

Things began to change in 2005, when my best friend took me to church.

The type of faith I heard about there was revolutionary. This church had people who had made big mistakes earlier in life but were loved, accepted, and fully involved. The God I met there accepted people as they were, in the midst of their brokenness.

This God wasn't out to judge. He wanted to love and transform. It was not about me reaching a set standard. It was about Him reaching me with a love that isn't conditional.

Love was a given.

God loved me despite my mess. Despite my failures. Despite the habits I was ashamed of. And He could use me, even in the midst of them.

My relationship with God was transformed. Revolutionised.

I began to grow in intimacy with God in a way I had not experienced before. And I was able to begin dealing with painful hurts from my past without fear. In this love, I was confronted with the truth of who I am—both positive and negative—and challenged to become transformed. In short, I joined a culture of grace: a community where I was free to be me.

I began to experience the depths of the grace that transforms.

What is the Grace that Transforms?

The grace that transforms is less afraid of God. Less anxious. Still challenged by God, but now able to have grown-up interactions with Him on a different level. God was no longer the class teacher scolding a disobedient child—but a loving Father talking with his son.

I'm still part of this same church today and continue to be confronted by new truths of who I am—both good and bad. I've experienced grace in this church more than in any other church I've been part of.

And I'm still being transformed.

But I know from my own upbringing, even into adulthood, that the experience of grace I've had in my current church isn't everyone's church experience. The "terror of the Lord" feeling, often disguised politely as "fear of the Lord," can be one of the biggest hindrances to us for understanding, receiving, and ultimately displaying God's grace.

You see, our view of God is fundamentally intertwined with how we experience and understand grace. Our God-view impacts our church life and our entire relationship with God. Our view has a direct impact on the lives of everyone around us.

Letting Go of Misconceptions

In order to trust God—experiencing grace, whatever our circumstance— we have to let go of our misconceptions and mistruths about God from experiences at churches or from our culture at large.

Ultimately, if we don't believe God is who He says He is—believing instead in some false idea of God—then our view of God is both inaccurate and rooted in a lie. And without truth, we can't be the people we were born to be.

Our view of God is never more clearly displayed than in times of suffering. Suffering exposes us, doesn't it? When conflict and disruption come into our lives, the truth of how we see God is exposed to the world.

Most of us have heard the phrase having to do with showing *grace under pressure.*

We can talk all we like about how much we trust God and how good God is. But if under pressure we react in a way that is completely contrary to trusting Him, then our words are hot air.

How many people do you know who talk about trusting God, who say that God is good, loving, and that they know and understand how precious they are to Him…but under pressure, these same people blame God for all that is wrong in their lives? They react to pain with bitterness, as if God is out to get them.

How many of us have done this exact thing?
(I think more of us than we would care to admit.)

I have my occasional rant at God, but after I've calmed down, I wonder what I was thinking. I know that what I said wasn't the truth. In fact, what I said about God hating me was a complete lie.

When conflict comes into my life, part of me still holds to the incorrect view that God is a distant deity waiting to hurt me, punish me, and make my life difficult—that He is part of some sick, divine scheme. This incorrect view that allows bitterness is much easier to believe than the truth.

Lies are often easier to believe than the truth, aren't they?

The strange thing is, I know the truth: God loves me. He's generous. He's forgiving. He's kind. He's good. He's full of grace. And I've experienced all of these qualities.

But when life struggles and conflicts come, I abandon the truth.

It's such a strange paradox.

Our life is such a journey. It is a process of understanding who God is and learning to live in the truth of His grace.

Be Prepared

Whenever we are under pressure, the old lies—mistruths we used to believe—tend to come back to us.

That's human nature.

It's easy to trust God when life is good. But once conflict comes, we are very quick to turn on Him, blame Him, and make accusations against Him. It's hard to believe the truth of a loving God when your mother dies, or when your best friend gets cancer. In such a broken, hurting world, it's just incredibly difficult to trust God.

I mean, let's be honest. It's really tough to trust God. I think very few of us can claim to trust God 100 percent.

Grace, played out in our lives, involves a process of learning to embrace the truth, even in horrible circumstances. It's letting grace transform you and me, even in the pain.

Grace Under Pressure

Hemingway famously said, "Courage is grace under pressure."[15] I agree, though I would take it further and say, "Faith is grace under pressure" because, in essence, *grace under pressure* refers to an ability to maintain calm, peace, and perspective under the most intense suffering. Faith is the same.

Faith is trusting God with the reality of our circumstances. It is acknowledging the truth and the reality of the situation we find ourselves in, whether that's the loss of job, a cancer diagnosis, an ongoing medical condition, or the loss of a loved one—and not letting the circumstances overwhelm you.

When you're in the midst of your darkest hour, when all hope seems gone

---

[15] The Hemingway quote, "Courage is grace under pressure," was first published in an April 20, 1926, letter Hemingway wrote F. Scott Fitzgerald. The letter is reprinted in *Ernest Hemingway: Selected Letters 1917-1961*, edited by Carlos Baker, pp. 199-201. Hemingway was also quoted in an article and profile piece in the New Yorker November 30, 1929, called "The Artist's Reward." You can find more info here, at http://www.sdiworld.org/about-us/tributes-memoriam/gerald-may-md.

and injustice abounds, it's much more difficult to say God is loving, good, and faithful than when things are going well.

Holding to grace and truth in all circumstances—especially when it's difficult, and despite all evidence to the contrary—is ultimately what real faith is all about.

It's a rare quality, one that's very difficult to attain.

Because trusting God is difficult.

Grace Under Pressure in My Own Life

People said that when my Mum died, I showed something akin to grace under pressure—that I was really strong about it. In one sense, I did trust God in that He had brought my Mum into eternity. But in another sense, I was burying my hurt and anger deep down, acting out of duty, not through faith or trust. In essence, the pain got in the way of fully accepting the grace.

It wasn't true grace under pressure.

The fact was that I was angry with God for taking my Mum away from me. I felt like He'd picked on me just like all the bullies at school had. How could God have allowed this to happen?

Have you ever asked that question? I bet so. We all do. We tend to trust God a lot less than we'd like to admit…which means we need grace more than ever.

Aspiring towards Grace

It's tough to achieve real grace under pressure, but we can aspire to it. Believe that God is a perfectly loving God: just, merciful, and forgiving. Believe that we are precious to Him. Under pressure, even when everything in life tells us otherwise, we must hold onto these truths.

This kind of faith has to be a conscious choice on our part. Intentional.

I have many friends who have achieved grace under pressure. Let me tell you about just two of them.

My first friend, Tanya, suffers from Myalgic Encephalomyelitis (ME), also known as chronic fatigue syndrome. To me, she is living proof of grace under pressure.

On one hand, she manages to own the truth of her situation, to not run from it…and yet, on the other hand, she somehow holds on, however scrappily, to the truth of who God is and what He says about her.

Tanya is daring to keep faith with Jesus when her circumstances give her every reason not to. She writes beautiful, poetic, wise blog posts pointing people towards Jesus, showing great faith, even in the midst of her own suffering. She is someone with great courage.

And in the exercise of her courage, I (and I'm sure many others) see God's grace.

My second friend, Joy, also has ME and writes amazing poetry. Even with ME, she still manages to continually promote and support others' work, encouraging all those she encounters—including me. She never gives up on God, no matter how much she struggles, and she inspires me with her level of faith and trust in God.

There are others I know who, in difficult circumstances, somehow manage to maintain faith despite all the negative they're experiencing. (Do you know people like this?)

These are people who struggle but who live greater lives through grace. They are fully aware of their reality but dare to trust in a God they believe-- deep in their bones-- to be good, loving, kind, and just. They trust in a God who weeps when we weep, is hurt when we hurt, and gets angry at the injustice in our lives and in His world.

This is the God I believe in. This is the God I trust in.

Despite my desires, I know my faith is weak. Maybe that's one reason Jesus said we only need mustard-seed sized faith: because true faith is so difficult to find.

But it can be found.

Living in faith, even under pressure, is a part of what grace is all about.

Chapter 7: Church
Honest Communities of Grace

"Imagine if every church became a place
where everyone is safe, but no one is comfortable.
Imagine if every church became a place
where we told one another the truth.
We might just create sanctuary."
Rachel Held Evans[16]

Different Views of God

Both inside and outside of the Christian church, there are many different views of God. When I talk to those outside the church about their view of God, there are two prevalent images that I come across.

The first is a "Distant Terror God": a God that is far away, physically and emotionally. This God is all-powerful, self-righteous, judgmental, and disconnected from the world. He allows unspeakable suffering to happen and waits for the opportunity to burn us all in hell.

The Distant Terror God demands way too much of us and threatens us with eternal torture if we don't agree and conform to His rules. The people who tell me of this type of God say, for the most part, that His followers are a bunch of self-righteous liars, hypocrites, religious nutters, and child abusers.

The other image of God is almost the opposite. I call this second view of God the "Santa-Claus God." We expect the Santa-Claus God to bless us all the time. He is the God of entitlement. He's also a God whose love for us is reflected only in the fact that He will give us exactly what we want, all the time. With Him, we get to live how we want to and do what we want to. And we expect God's blessing when we need it.

When life is good, people forget the Santa-Claus God. When things go badly, they get angry with Him because they didn't receive what they

---

[16] Rachel Held Evans, *Searching for Sunday: Loving, Leaving, and Finding the Church*, p. 73.

believe they should have. They believe that God has failed them. Those believing in the Santa-Claus God automatically assume when things go wrong that this God is punishing them. It's tempting, then, to think that God is being vindictive, maybe even malicious.

It's very easy to get angry with a god like this.

There's no real relationship involved with the Santa-Claus view of God, apart from when things go wrong. When things are good, there's no need to bother talking to Him (outside of asking for blessings). When things are bad, there's no real dialogue with this God, either. Overall, the Santa-Claus God is not built on a relationship of interaction together. He's essentially a Vending Machine God. We take what we need from Him and ignore or reject Him when we don't need Him.

Do either of these views of God—Distant Terror God or Santa-Claus God—sound familiar to you?

Essentially, the Distant Terror God sends His Son to rescue us from His wrath, from burning in hell forevermore. On the other hand, the Santa-Claus God is someone we take from, as much as it suits us.

It's all about what we deserve, or don't deserve.

With the Distant Terror God, when we suffer, we deserve to suffer. With the Santa-Claus God, when we suffer, we don't deserve to suffer.

Grace doesn't fit either of these views.

Which means that, in large part, grace has been lost.

(By the way, you probably guessed it: I don't believe in either of these "gods.")

In our consumer society, grace is not often spoken of. That's because a consumer society is all about merit. It's about what you can earn. You work hard because you are gifted or skilled, and you most likely get the financial rewards.

But a consumer society is also about *lack*. It's about what we don't have, as well as what we need. It's about getting the material products that will make you and me "feel all right" in the end.

Both *merit* and *lack* imply that you and I have to earn our way into happiness, fulfilment, and acceptance. It's not a gift.

That leaves grace out.

The only grace many of us hear about in church has to do with happy-clappy, smiley-faced Christians who speak only Christianese (Christian vernacular) and is, in truth, disconnected from reality.

Christianese unto itself isn't bad. Sometimes it's easier to speak with terms that we all know. But there's no doubt in my mind that followers of Jesus use Christianese way too much. (I'm as guilty as anyone.)

The problem is, when we use Christianese, we can forget the real meaning of the words that we're using.

"Redeemed"
"Salvation"
"The Gospel"
"Sin"
"Repentance"

Do these words have power for us? Do these words sound fresh and life giving?

Though powerful, these words can be emptied of their meaning and redefined to fit the shallow image of the happy-clappy Christian, which is a tragedy. Christianese and false views of God perpetuated by some can disconnect the church from everyone else outside of the church—doing incalculable damage to the name of Jesus.

The Church

The problem is, the Christian church doesn't do enough to dispel the Distant Terror or the Santa-Claus God myths—or the rampant use of Christianese. Christians can be accused of being hypocrites. And you know what? The accusations can be correct.

All of us—Christian and non-Christian alike—are hypocrites. We all make mistakes. None of us live out our beliefs perfectly.

It's true: Church leaders have committed unspeakable acts of abuse and torture over the centuries and covered it up. Like you, I feel disgusted and uncomfortable that people who claim to believe in the God of love, grace, and mercy have abused their position. This isn't the way of Jesus, in any shape or form.

The Church hasn't done its job. The false impressions of God push people away. Our lack of living in true relationship in grace pushes people away.

A Place of Secrets

Another problem is that many churches have become places where secrets are kept—or perhaps better stated, kept out.

Many churches have become places where people are too afraid to be honest about their fears, doubts, and insecurities. Even issues such as abuse and sexuality can be kept hidden, for fear of the consequences.

Often, when a church is planted, it's a small group out to change the world and politics don't come into the picture. The people in the church have nothing to lose, nothing to protect, and are often more willing to take big risks and receive all types of people into the group—openly and honestly.

Some churches have a desire to become as big as possible, being receptive to as many people as possible. Suddenly, people have their "own" ministries. Committees, trustees, elders, politics, and people have "kingdoms" to lose.

As the church gets bigger, we want to please everyone. We want to try to not offend, especially those who are the biggest givers of money to the church. And as they grow, churches are tempted to not tackle difficult topics—because, again, they have more to lose.
I'm not trying to generalize…but such issues can be big problems in our churches.

Church is a place where we should be able to be open and completely honest. We need to be able to honestly talk about what's really going on in our lives—without judgment or exclusion and without shame.

It's a place where we should be accepted, no matter our struggle.

A safe place.

The Problem of the Mask

Instead of providing safety for authenticity, churches can become places where people put on masks.

People often feel that they're not able to be fully themselves. They're afraid. It's an atmosphere that runs under the surface and is not spoken about. But it's real.

We tend to hide our mistakes, failures, embarrassments, broken lives, and dark secrets. We don't disclose weaknesses and needs because we're afraid we'll become disconnected from the rest of the church. We may feel we'll lose our reputation or our ministry.

This isn't a home for grace. It's a home for fear. That's not how Jesus intended the church to be.

Church must be a community of people journeying through life together, learning the way of Jesus, and feeling completely safe to be ourselves— with all our mistakes—yet knowing we're loved, accepted, and able to live in healthy community together.

You can find positive atmospheres of community outside the religious establishment. A form of "church" doesn't happen only with people who believe in God. "Community" can happen without God, as in a gathering of people together where you're loved and accepted as you are. But to have authentic *Christian* community, we have to have Jesus in the centre.

An internationally known author told a story about encountering this kind of church.[17] When he first became a pastor, a member of his church came

---

[17] This story comes from a conference with Rob Bell that I attended in 2015.

up to him after a service and said, "If you want to see 'real church,' go to an AA [Alcoholics Anonymous] meeting." So he went.

The first thing he noticed was a sign over the entrance that said, "No Bullshit." Though that's a brash statement, the point is, the AA meeting is designed to be an honest, accepting place without falsity and lies. With hope. And full of grace.

Honesty, acceptance, and hope are exactly what church should be.

The message of AA is clear: this is who I am. I'm going to take the steps to deal with it. And even as I am, I'm still a valuable person. I don't have to prove myself, or earn anyone else's approval, to be loved and accepted.

Christ earned salvation for us, and Jesus' sacrifice is at the heart of the gospel. We are accepted because of His sacrifice on the cross, taking the punishment we deserve. God *is* a God of Justice, but we receive mercy through Christ.

Isn't that the heart of the gospel?

No hiding. No being polite in front of people. No disguising our weaknesses. Not acting out of self-protection. Owning who we really are. Being vulnerable. Admitting our dark side.

A Christian community has Christ at the centre, so while AA might fall short of being a church, AA is a great example of how grace transforms. It can also be a good model for how church should be: a place where we don't feel the need to hide anything for the sake of appearances. No disguising weaknesses. A space without fear of full disclosure.

Despite how wonderful my church is, I can at times find it difficult to discuss my most shameful habits there. It has nothing to do with the atmosphere in the church and everything to do with a fear that was ingrained into me from previous church experiences.

Plus, of course, it's just human nature to hide our weaknesses.

Culture tells us life is all about winning, about being the best and not showing weakness. And even though we try to avoid the stories that culture tells us, it's difficult not to be impacted by them.

It's easy for us to think we have to live up to a certain standard. We can feel it even more so in a church context. We look at people around us and think they have their lives together. So it's easy to feel like we have to act all together, too.

At the core, we're afraid. Afraid that if we admit our weaknesses, then the people we love will reject us. That our church leaders will reject us. And somehow, God will reject us.

Pride can also be at the centre of this fear of honesty. Admitting weakness means admitting that we cannot save ourselves, and it's impossible to be prideful and accept grace.

No matter the cause, churches have become a home for secrets rather than spaces for us to be vulnerable. They've become organisations brushing mistakes and issues under the carpet rather than confronting them.

We might be afraid to admit we've been divorced or abused. There are plenty of stories with women afraid to admit abuse by their husband or another man because the church leader said it's not "honouring their husband" to talk or respond.

This is unhealthy and a culture of judgment. It's a culture of fear—or rather, terror. Nowhere near a culture of grace.

If we're in a church where we're afraid to be honest about our shadow side and about difficult issues going on in our lives, then perhaps we're not in a church that's following the way of Jesus.

A Metaphor

I heard a great metaphor from church in a blog post I read recently, how churches can become like crack dens.[18]

Sound strange? The point is that people can go to church to get a "spiritual hit" for the week.
The rest of the week, there's no real relationship or discipleship—true personal growth and accountability while connecting with others. It's just a weekly adrenaline and supernatural rush to (hopefully) make us happy and content for a week.

So here's another even more challenging question: Do we go to church to keep God off our back?

Recently, I watched someone hurriedly, apologetically, and with a sense of panic, apologise to the pastor for not being in church the previous week.

Why would this person apologise? If you or I think God is a God of Terror just waiting to punish us for not keeping the right religious rules, then missing church becomes a legitimate fear. We're going to church as a way of appeasing God.

Examining *why* we go to church can open up a whole different perspective, one that can help deepen our relationship with God.

My Story

When I was a teenager, I went to church to appease God and to make sure I was right with Him so I wouldn't be in too much trouble. Going to church was about doing the right thing, so God would be pleased with me. In hindsight, that wasn't healthy at all.

When I went to university, I discovered a different God. A God who was up close and intimate, who met me in power and made me feel a presence and a peace I'd never known. I fell in love with this God. I wanted to be

---

[18] Peter Rollins, from http://peterrollins.net/2012/03/the-contemporary-church-is-a-crack-house/, accessed May 20, 2016.

with Him all the time. I began going to church out of a love for God, not a duty to God—or in fear of consequences.

And then, a few years later, I began realising my passion for God had gone. I wasn't experiencing God as I had been, at first. Why wasn't I experiencing God in my every-day life? Where had He gone?

One Sunday, I got the answer.

During the service and in the prayer time afterwards, I had a sense that God was speaking to me. It's a not an audible voice, and it's not an emotional feeling. It's a deep, meaningful thought, coupled with a sense in my soul. I can't explain it adequately in words, as it's very personal. But God made it very clear that I'd been treating church as my spiritual hit for the week. I'd begun going to church out of obligation, in the knowledge that I'd get spiritually fed there.

I had left God at church and stopped trying to meet with God in my own time. Church had become my spiritual crack den.

I'd become what I'd detested over the years: a Sunday Christian. My reasons for going to church were way out of sync. I needed to take action, to change.

Church should never be the place we go to get our dose of God for the week. And it should never be a place we go to appease God, either. Neither of these perspectives is healthy, and neither spring from a view of God rooted in grace.

The view of God as a terrifying, wrathful being out to get us leads to the appeasement approach. The crack-den view of church as a spiritual hit comes from the Santa-Claus view of God: God will bless us and give us what we need in our weekly dose when we go to Him to get what we need.

Why do We Go to Church?

The reason to go to church should never be fear, and it should never be simply to get blessed. No, church is about growing in faith in community. Church is meant to be a safe place, to be vulnerable before God and others about whom you are, to be challenged and become disciples (followers of Jesus who are committed to learning and growing), and to know the love and grace of God. A place where you know you are accepted as you are, and safe to be honest about your brokenness.

In AA, the beginning of the process of change is about owning up to your shadow. Everyone else hears about your issue, and no one sits in judgment on anyone else—because everyone else has the same issue.

This is a perfect model for church.

Okay, in church, we may not have the same issues—but we all have ways we've disconnected from God. We all have issues where we need healing and transformation. All of us need forgiveness.

Jesus calls us to live through the lens of grace. He calls us to love one another, not to judge one another.

When a couple is intimate sexually, they are physically naked with one another, the most vulnerable you can possibly be. No hiding anything. Because in a healthy marriage there is complete trust between each partner and seeing each other naked—scars, belly, moles, and all. It is an act of complete vulnerability and trust.

A church where secrets are kept is like a couple that keeps their clothes on, never seeing each other naked. It's a couple without trust, keeping secrets from each other and, in essence, afraid of being vulnerable with one another.

Is that a healthy picture of marriage? Of course, not.

Our Relationship to God

According to the Scriptures, our relationship with God is compared to a marriage. In fact, God calls His church the "Bride of Christ."[19] God loves us and wants us to be vulnerable with Him. A relationship with

---

[19] The phrase, "Bride Of Christ," isn't a specific quote out of the bible but is a metaphor of the church as the bride and Jesus as the bridegroom, as found in John 3:29, Mark 2:19.

Jesus is a safe place to be vulnerable—and this is precisely what healthy expressions of church must be. Imagine a group where you had no choice but to confront yourself completely and to publicly shine a light on your dark side. But even further, imagine a community where you could do this without fear. No fear of exposing your dark side. No fear of any consequences, for being vulnerable.

A space that was so full of love, grace, forgiveness and trust, no one was ever afraid to share absolutely *anything*.

A space where you can be honest with God and others about your doubts, fears, and questions about faith—and take time to honestly explore those thoughts and questions in a healthy way.

A place you can get angry when the one you love dies from cancer.

A place where you can tell God what you really think of Him and how you feel about the pain going on around you.

A community where you can cry out and question God about the incredible injustices we see all around us. Injustices that can rightly make us question whether God even loves us or takes any notice.

And a place where we can honestly express our greatest desires and craziest dreams, our yearnings for how we hope life will go.

Can you imagine a church where these things actually happened?

The True Church

Imagine a place where, no matter what we shared, unconditional love and acceptance was there, waiting. In this safe place, the past would not be held against any person. The community would focus on helping each of us deal with both darkness and joy.

Overcoming an addiction.
Coping with a broken marriage or relationship.
Admitting suicidal thoughts.
Confessing a fault, a challenge, a failure, but still feeling safe.

A community like this is precisely what Jesus meant by church.

I'll be honest: This kind of church excites me. It's the kind of church I'd like to be part of.

Can you imagine it?
Does it exist?

I think it could. In fact, I am sure there are places like this out there. My church is the closest I've experienced to it.

Is it scary? Yes.
Is it comfortable? No.

Because as we've seen, grace isn't always comfortable. Grace rips us apart and exposes the truth of who we are. This is what discipleship is. It's what happens in church.

Real church brings real transformation.

Real discipleship occurs where people confront the hard issues and are truly healed of deep hurts from the past. Where people can experience the deepest depths of grace and become restored. It's a place where we display the shattered glass of our lives.

And then, together with God and others, slowly but surely, we piece it back together, to create a beautiful mosaic.

In short, this kind of church is the kingdom of God. Here, now.

Chapter 8: Edge
Grace's Two-Sided Blade

"I do not at all understand the mystery of grace—
only that it meets us where we are
but does not leave us where it found us."
Anne Lamott[20]

We've seen that grace is fundamental to how we see and understand God. We've examined how important it is to have grace with ourselves. And we've explored how grace is fundamental to how we do church. But to understand and experience the true depths of grace, and become people of grace ourselves, we have to go deeper.

There's a dangerous side of grace we haven't encountered yet.

Dangerous Grace

Grace has a dark side to it. And I'm not talking about Star Wars.

If we truly want to experience the depths of grace, we need to recognise that grace has an edge. And that edge is sharp.

Grace's sharp edge cuts like a knife deep into the heart of who we are, often into the areas we want to ignore. This process[21] cuts into the habits, actions, and decisions that are not helping others. It cuts into the areas where we are not blessing God and into where we're doing damage to ourselves.

Grace may not feel good.

If grace is only about feeling good, about happiness and celebration, that grace is (as we've said before) like the resurrection without the crucifixion. It means nothing.

---

[20] *Traveling Mercies: Some Thoughts on Faith*, Anchorbooks.com (1999), p. 143.

[21] The church calls this process *sanctification*.

A tea bowl needs to be broken before it becomes a beautiful piece of Kintsugi. In the same way, we must allow ourselves to be broken before we can experience the true depths and transforming power of grace.

We need to experience the edge of grace.

Grace that Cuts but Transforms

Let me tell you about my best friend, Dog (believe it or not, that's his real nickname). Dog gave me permission to share his story, hoping others would learn from his mistakes.

Dog is without doubt one of the best (and one of most unique) men I've ever met. He's a man who challenged me to come out of my comfort zone in every possible sense. When we first met, we hated each other. He was the rebel in our group of friends, and I was the goody two-shoes. He used to wind me up something chronic—and by all accounts, I wound him up, too.

So in many ways, it was almost destined that we would become best friends.

Dog went away to work as a Youth Worker in northern England, on a contract for a minimum of five years. Part of his work was to integrate himself into drug communities and build relationships with the intention of sharing his faith. The only problem was, Dog became too integrated. He developed a serious drug problem himself, which also drove him deep into debt. I never knew exactly how bad Dog's problem became, but I knew it was very, very serious.

Then grace stepped in.

Sometimes when we hear the word "then," we immediately believe we're skipping to the happy ending. But grace doesn't skip. It's not as simple as that. For Dog, when grace stepped in, life became worse. He lost himself and was almost without hope. As with all of us, his choices had consequences, and even before he'd been in northern England a year, he lost his job. The dream became a nightmare.

Dog knew life couldn't go on as it was. He had to do something. So he committed to giving up the drugs. People who loved him paid off his debt, and Dog agreed to pay these people back. He got a job back home and he began his life again.

It was at this point that we became close friends.

I saw something in Dog, even when we didn't like each other, which interested me. Dog had a fire in his belly. He didn't want to be like everyone else and just follow the status quo. When Dog's mind was focused in the right areas, I saw that he could achieve great things.

I began to see a change in Dog that only grace could make.

You know, at the start, Dog serving the drug community looked great on the outside. It appeared that Dog had embraced his calling. But it really wasn't that way.

We all do that sometimes, don't we? On the outside, we appear to have it all together. But on the inside, we're not confronting the truth.

We can use activities—work, family, church, or education (anything, really)—to cover up our weaknesses and avoid confronting the real issues. But we need to confront the weaknesses, or they'll keep coming back.

Dog came to the absolute end of himself. When he had nothing left, he confronted the uncomfortable truth about his life and committed to change.

And change he did.

Transformation that's Real

He was transformed. A forward momentum began driving his life. He took responsibility in his work and found himself promoted. He found the committed love of a girlfriend who became his wife. And above all, he grew in faith more than ever before. He served in church, became involved in leadership, and began to inspire many people, including me.

Indeed, it was because of Dog that I found my current church. He had discovered this church and thought it was amazing. It was clear that Dog was undergoing tremendous growth through this church community. So I went along with Dog to his church. And immediately, I felt the Spirit of God telling me that this church was home. I was where I was meant to be.

Soon enough, I was in the church and growing too, seeing more of Dog's growth at first hand.

Exposing Ourselves to Grace's Edge

Dog had, in his lowest, darkest moment, exposed himself to the edge of grace. Instead of hiding what he had done, trying to escape the pain and its consequences, Dog chose instead to allow grace to cut him open.

Through grace, Dog exposed the ugly truth and looked square at it. Like a surgeon who cuts open the chest for heart surgery, he saw the heart. Exposing what's truly wrong, instead of hiding it, allowed the core problems and issues to be dealt with.

As Dog received the grace that's painful, the grace of exposure, it was undoubtedly a highly uncomfortable experience. But it was only in that discomfort that Dog began to be transformed.

It was my honour to be the best man on Dog's wedding day. It was a day of true joy and celebration—for the wedding celebration itself *and* because the wedding was, in truth, the marking point of his transformed life, a celebration of how far he'd come. All because Dog had confronted his life with the edge of grace.

If we don't face grace's edge, there will always be issues holding us back— the habits, bad attitudes, insecurities, and mistakes that we try to hide from. If we ignore the problems, the problems and issues can begin to control us.

Dog's story perfectly illustrates how grace transforms. And if we are to be the people God created us to be, we too must expose ourselves to the edge of grace.

James Prescott

A Story from the Bible

The Bible has something to say about this kind of transforming grace.

In John's account of Jesus' life, Jesus tells a story about throwing stones. It revolves largely around a woman caught in adultery.

Though our present-day society of "anything goes" says that adultery is something that people justify or even accept, many of us would agree that being unfaithful to a spouse is not loving or ethical.

In Jesus' time, the same sentiment was strong—so strong that a suitable punishment for adultery was stoning a person to death. Of course, that's barbaric for us, today. And it was barbaric and unacceptable for Jesus, as well.

Make no mistake: The woman was not innocent. She was caught in the act. There was no way she could run away from her actions and no chance to deny her guilt. And everyone knew it. She was confronted with her own brokenness in front of everyone.

So the religious leaders—the Pharisees—brought the adulterous woman to Jesus.

The Pharisees heard about Jesus and His teaching, and they wanted to put Jesus to the test in order to expose Him as a fraud. Probably, in all honesty, the Pharisees wanted to show how righteous they were compared to this woman.

If Jesus had actually stoned her to death along with the Pharisees, the Pharisees wouldn't have condemned Jesus for it because they thought stoning was the righteous thing to do. (Following this harsh law was what was expected of anyone, including Jesus).

In fact, if Jesus had stoned the woman, He might have been accepted by more people—at least by the Pharisees. Let's be honest. If we found out that someone had been unfaithful to us, or to a close friend, would we feel sorry for the person caught?

Really?

No. We'd be upset. Hurt. Angry even.

Essentially, we'd want some kind of judgment on that person. Deep inside, we'd want condemnation. Justice. Retribution.

It would take time for us to forgive the person who wronged us in such a terrible way.

This is probably how people felt in relation to the woman in the story. Indeed, it's how the whole community seemed to be feeling.

If we were in this situation, either then or in a modern context, then there is every chance we'd want the woman punished. Not by stoning, of course. But we'd want some kind of justice. At the very least, we'd want her to take responsibility for what happened.

Now, on top of this, the woman was a social outcast. The lowest of the low. Someone almost unforgivable.

Imagine who that person is in your life.

The person who assaulted or abused you.
The partner who cheated on you.
The person who betrayed your trust.
The person who hurt you the most.

And you'll have a picture of how this woman was looked upon.

Many of us have been betrayed by those we've trusted. And even if we like to brush over the pain, it's there, deep in our soul.

The parent who hit us.
The bully who didn't stop.
The boss who put us down.
The person who raped or abused us.

And often, it's easier to *not* forgive.

In culture, some offences are deemed unforgivable. We often believe that the people who have hurt us deeply—or who have hurt those we love—

James Prescott

don't deserve our sympathy. They don't deserve forgiveness. We believe this perspective is understandable and acceptable

Because who wants to forgive an abuser?
And why should they deserve forgiveness?

No, they should get what they deserve.
There's no reason for us to forgive them.
We have the right to revenge.

Don't we?

With the adulterous woman in Jesus' time, it would have been acceptable to most people for them to stone her. No one would have blamed Jesus for allowing her to be stoned.

Yet Jesus didn't judge her.
He didn't condemn her.
He didn't punish her.

What did He do?

He forgave her.

He released her from condemnation.

No more was she bound by what she had done.
The acts she had committed were in the past.
Gone.
Wiped out.
Forgotten.

No revenge.

And this is simply scandalous.

Jesus sets free a woman essentially condemned to death for her actions. Jesus, the only perfect human being—the only man qualified to judge and condemn her—doesn't condemn her.

Instead, He says, "Neither do I condemn you. Go."[22]

I believe that not condemning the woman who is so obviously guilty is one of the most underestimated acts in Scripture.

We may not understand the gravity of the act she committed and the scandal Jesus' words caused. It's the same as Jesus going to the most unforgivable person you can imagine, the people you hate and think deserve punishment, and saying to them, *I don't condemn you.*

Do you get how massive this is?

And notice what *isn't* said. (This is big.) The woman *doesn't repent.* She *doesn't apologize.* She *doesn't show remorse.* She's completely silent.

Most amazingly, Jesus doesn't wait for her to repent. In the midst of her brokenness, He loves her, accepts her, and forgives her. Right where she is. *As she is.*

Because His acceptance of her is not based on anything she does. It's unconditional.

It's a gift.

This challenges me. It should challenge all of us.

In scripture, Jesus tells His disciples—the people who want to follow His way, then and now—to *love one another.*

We often talk about how we are meant to love one another unconditionally, but in reality, it becomes...

Love one another *as long as you're like me or love me back.*
Love one another *as long as you haven't hurt me.*
Love one another *but not if you're a murderer or abuser.*
It's easier to love those who love us. And it's natural to despise—or even hate—those who have hurt us—those people guilty of what society deems

---

[22] "No one, sir," she said. "Then neither do I condemn you," Jesus declared. "Go now and leave your life of sin." John 8:11, New International Version, the Bible.

unforgivable offences.

Love with addendums is often the way of the world.

A New Way

But Jesus comes and tells us differently. He demonstrates unconditional love more than once—not just with this woman caught in adultery but also on the cross itself.

Jesus was tortured to within an inch of His life. He had to carry a heavy beam of wood, a cross. And after carrying the beam, he hung from that cross, dying. Alone and abandoned by those He knew. And above all, unjustly convicted. Innocent but sentenced to death.

Next to Him was a criminal. A murderer. An outcast who was guilty as charged and getting the lawful punishment for his crime. Someone most of us would reject.

The criminal dared to ask Jesus one simple thing: "Lord, remember me."

The criminal knew he had no right to ask for anything. But he stepped out in faith to ask Jesus to remember Him. Does Jesus ignore the outcast? Does He reject him? Does He tell the murderer he's getting what he deserves, and he's going to hell because of it?

No.

Jesus said, "Today, you will be with me in paradise."[23]

Even on the cross, Jesus didn't condemn. He didn't stand in judgment. He simply loved, forgave, and extended grace—even to the most evil of us.

To those hated by the world.
The murderers. The rapists. The abusers. Those who commit unspeakable acts towards the vulnerable. Yes, you read that correctly. Jesus loves them.

---

[23] "Jesus answered him, 'Truly I tell you, today you will be with me in paradise.'" Luke 32:43, New International Version, the Bible.

And today, if any of these outcasts asked Jesus to remember them, He would.

Kerry's Story

Dog was one example of redemption. Now I'd like to talk briefly about a woman I'll call Kerry (which is not her real name).

When she was 16 years old, Kerry was cruelly and violently attacked with a knife by two men. But the knife attack was not the end. They took her, shoved her into a car, and forced themselves on her. Again and again. For hours. It was horrific, terrifying, and left painful physical and emotional scars. Kerry decided the best way to deal with her pain was to simply ignore it, and she began a new life.

When Kerry began a relationship with a Christian man, it started out well. But she developed a physical condition that caused cancer and infertility. The dream of having children with the Christian man she loved was shattered. Worse yet, it was found that the condition was directly caused by that night of abuse.

Facing up to the pain of the past, Kelly began to suffer from issues relating to shame, fear, and low self-esteem. At the same time, she began chemotherapy.

Kerry had every reason to never forgive her attackers for the way they violently robbed her of her innocence and sabotaged forever her chance to have children. No one would have blamed Kerry if she never forgave her attackers. If you or the person you love the most was abused like Kerry and suffered the same consequences, would you forgive?

I can't honestly say whether I would or wouldn't. I don't know.

Our culture would say that rapists don't deserve forgiveness. That we should let them be punished, disconnecting them from the wider world and giving them the worst possible punishment, even death. Forgiveness would not even remotely be considered.

But a lack of forgiveness has a price.

The longer Kerry held on to the past and refused to forgive, the more she found that the un-forgiveness held her back and stopped her from truly living. In reality, un-forgiveness brought increasing anger, resentment, and bitterness. The longer the bitterness went on, the bigger the disconnection between her and God became. The abuse that took her innocence and robbed her of children now threatened to ruin her relationship with God.

But this wasn't the end.

Kerry realised how the pain controlled her, and God led Kerry to a place where she could let go of the past and surrender it to Him. It was a process that took time, reflection, and prayer. It didn't happen overnight.

She began to forgive the men.

Not long into the process of forgiveness, Kerry prayed for a woman in her church. It turned out this woman was the mother of her abusers. When Kerry found out, she didn't feel the anger she'd felt before. And at that moment, she realised in her heart that she had actually forgiven the men. It was something that had happened almost subconsciously, over time.

With the realization, Kerry felt freer than ever before.

She had forgiven the unforgivable. She had let go of the past, let go of her right to revenge, and chose to love instead.

This is a rare story.

This kind of forgiveness is scandalous in our culture. There are many who might even be angry with Kerry because they believe she's letting the abusers have power over her by forgiving them.

Actually, she is doing the exact opposite.

The Power of Forgiveness

When we forgive, we take power away from horrific actions and the people responsible for them. We're set free from the past.

Jesus calls us to make the scandalous choice of forgiveness.

When He says, "I do not condemn you," he is saying the words to all—even the "unforgiveable people." He is saying, "I love you, even exposed. Even in your brokenness. Even in the mess of your present life. Despite what you have done…I love you."

That kind of grace makes the phrase *amazing grace* almost insufficient.

Let's not get confused, though. I'm not saying that people like the men who raped Kerry should get away scot-free. Grace *isn't* about letting people off the hook. It requires us to take responsibility and does not exclude us from the consequences of our actions. Responsibility and consequences are necessary and should be enforced, as a society.

I'm saying that Kerry, as an individual, was free to let go of the bondage of the pain.

Grace calls us to love those who the world hates. To love those who maybe even we feel anger and hatred towards. You and I can extend love and forgiveness yet still hold the person accountable for his or her actions.

This is the edge of grace.
The scandal of grace.
The counter-cultural call of Christ to His people.

And it's shocking. It's unfair. It can make us angry.

But Grace isn't meant to be fair. Grace is meant to be good.

We have to confront the edge of grace—the uncomfortable quality of grace—in order to receive it, be transformed by it, and share it with others.

James Prescott

Confrontation Transformation

Dog didn't hide from the consequences of his actions. He faced them, took responsibility for them, and committed to a new life. And as he received grace, it began to pour into the lives of others—including me.

Kerry confronted the truth of her abusers. Jesus loved, accepted, and forgave the woman caught in adultery. Like Jesus, Kerry extended grace to the unforgiveable.

In the raw, painful confrontation, grace is extended. It has an edge that both hurts and heals, taking us to a place beyond what we can normally do.

If you've made a mistake, receive the truth that you're forgiven. If you're the victim, you can learn to forgive the people who've hurt you. And in the process, your hurt can be healed. Either way, it's about forgiveness. Either way, you receive grace. You find healing.

But there's more.

Here's the Secret:

When we expose ourselves to the edge of grace, we see that we are loved more than we ever imagined. A truth is revealed—that we are not only broken, but also that God *already knew this.*

And in His knowing, He loves us infinitely, unconditionally, and wonderfully in that place.

The edge of grace reveals to us just how much we are loved in our mess. Grace is not love with conditions or love only when we have it all together.
It's not love when we get our lives in order or only when we do things correctly.
It's not being loved only when we believe the right things.

It is God loving us even when we hated God.
It is God loving us when we hurt another person.
It is God loving us when we were in the midst of that addiction.

It is God loving us when we were in the worst place.
It is God loving us when we didn't even believe God existed.

And this love is beautiful.

As we open ourselves to the edge of grace, we allow a wave of the infinite love of God to break over our hearts and fill us up. We feel a peace, a joy, and (above all) a grace like we've never known.

In such grace, we are never the same again.

Grace may be a gift from God. But it's not easy. It's not instant. It's not simple. It's not comfortable.

It's grace with a beautiful edge.

Chapter 9: Cost
Aware of Grace's Disruption

"Cheap grace is the deadly enemy of the church."
Dietrich Bonhoeffer[24]

A couple of years back, some friends and I committed to reading one Psalm per day and read to the end of the Book of Psalms. Once the Psalms were finished, I began another book. And then read another. Each morning, I kept on with my study.

But then "life got in the way."

My sister came to stay with me, which disrupted my life. I didn't read my Bible. In reality, my stopping had nothing to do with my sister, because I could have read in my bedroom. I just made the excuse that, because I couldn't read where I normally did, I wouldn't be able to read at all that day. And I told myself that my sister would be moving out relatively quickly anyway, so I could pick up the Bible reading again when she left.

The problem is, I got out of the habit of reading. Once out of the habit, it was much easier to forget completely about it. Eventually, I wasn't getting positive input into my life.

And I realised there was one other, more significant reason that I stopped reading, too.

The previous year had been a tough time for me, filled with insecurities, fears, and doubts. The devotions and Bible passages during this time had been a lifeline to me. They had kept me on track.

But life had changed for the better. I'd gone through that dark time and come out the other side. I'd experienced a deep, transforming grace in my life, and life was looking positive. So when life was going well again (I'd come through the hardship and survived), I felt weird inside.

---

[24] *The Cost of Discipleship* (1963), New York, NY: Macmillan Publishing Co., p. 45.

Weird. There's no other way to describe it. After being stuck in the middle of my parents' divorce, struggling with the memories of negative circumstances for over a decade, and going through losing a parent, suddenly, life was good. My writing was taking off, church was going spectacularly well, and work was fine, with the potential for promotion. Relationships were good, and there was, for the first time, a woman in my life.

I was the one being blessed. I looked at my life and realised how fortunate I was, and how gracious God had been to me.

One of the first things I said to God was, "God, please don't let me take my circumstances for granted. In case I forget to tell you in the future, I want you to know how thankful I am for what you've given me."

Taking Goodness for Granted

But of course, in subsequent weeks, I did take circumstances for granted. It was easier to give up devotionals and Bible studies because, when things were going well, I wasn't dependent on them so much.

I'd experienced the depths of God's grace in my life, and now I was cheapening that grace by taking it for granted.

I was reaping the blessings of God in my life and forgetting the cost.

I wasn't making sacrifices for God. I wasn't being disciplined. And I wasn't taking responsibility for my faith in my daily life.

Part of my taking God for granted was simply due to the fact that I wasn't used to being in the place of blessing. It was like going to your dream holiday destination: you've dreamt about going, but even when you get there, you still can't quite believe it's real—and you're not sure how to act.

Realising I had forgotten the true cost of His forgiveness, His mercy, and His transforming work in my life was quite sobering. I looked at myself and saw a spoilt brat, someone who had taken these hard earned, precious gifts and abused them, neglecting the very One who had shed blood to win them.

It was then that I was reminded of one simple truth.

Grace isn't Cheap. It's Costly.

As you and I begin to know God's goodness to us, life can begin to go well and circumstances improve. When life is good, we can forget what we had to go through to get there.

And if grace costs us nothing, it's not grace at all.

Alternatively, we can ignore transformation and go on with our lives as they were before. We can simply pay a token acknowledgement to God's forgiveness and healing, moving on without tangible growth in our lives.

At that point, I question whether a person understands grace, because if you or I have truly received grace, then we'll be transformed.

Grace doesn't suddenly solve our problems. But there are times that you and I come out on the other side and we're not just surviving, but thriving. Taking the thriving for granted, not appreciating the gift that it is, cheapens our lives.

In all circumstances, grace is costly.

The Cost of Discipleship

In the 1930s, up against the backdrop of the rise of Nazi Germany, Dietrich Bonhoeffer wrote a book called, *The Cost of Discipleship*. In 1943, Bonhoeffer was eventually arrested and then in 1945, just before the liberation (at the age of 39), was executed by the Nazis.

In his book, Bonhoeffer wrote about cheap grace. The chapter on cheap grace is worth the price of the book on it's own, in my estimation.

Cheap grace, he argued, is grace without discipleship. Cheap grace gives forgiveness without repentance; baptism without church discipline; and forgets about discipleship. In other words, cheap grace simply says *yes* to God, getting all the benefits of the cross, without the cost.

Bonhoeffer also wrote, "Cheap grace is the enemy of the church."[25]

We can't be a church that cheapens grace or a culture that takes the cross of Jesus for granted, spending endless amounts of time in only celebrating God. We must have balance—recognising what He has brought us through, with gratitude. Gratitude brings joy into our lives and leads us to worship. Understanding God's deep, unconditional grace is at the core of true worship.

Grace comes through disruption. When we allow grace to bring us through an area where we've struggled—confronting a difficult truth about ourselves or about some kind of traumatic event—grace infiltrates our hearts, transforms us, and heals us.

As a result, you and I experience true joy and gratitude.

In contrast, cheap grace is one-dimensional. There's no sacrifice, commitment, or cost on our part. Cheap grace worships, praises, and feels good without confronting the world we live in.

Cheap grace paints a picture of a world where everything is happy. Every problem in this life is resolved—or at least can be—through prayer.

Cheap grace refuses to acknowledge the real problems in our world.

Cheap grace doesn't engage with the people who Jesus truly wants to reach: the broken, the messed up, and the lonely. The people who don't always get their prayers answered, to whom life is consumed with one disaster after another. These are the social outcasts, the ones the world forgets.

We can't afford to look away from those persons whose prayers don't appear to be answered. Prayers aren't always answered the way we desire them to be. People aren't always healed when we pray for them. That's reality.

---

[25] Deitrich Bonhoeffer, *Costly Grace*, p. 43, as translated by R. H. Fuller, with some revision by Irmgard Booth (1959), noted https://en.wikiquote.org/wiki/Dietrich_Bonhoeffer#Costly_Grace.

James Prescott

We can easily live off cheap grace. Many do. We try to brush the harsh realities of life under the carpet, not acknowledging real problems that real people carry every day. Many of us live the consumer dream, listening to stories of success and achievement.

We are blind to what grace can do around us.

The Prodigal Son

Jesus tells a story of a son who went to his father, telling the father he wanted his inheritance right then and there.[26] In essence, the son acted like his father was of no worth, other than the wealth that the father could leave the son. So the father divided his inheritance between the younger son (who wanted to leave) and his eldest son.

Sure enough, the younger son left with the money—and promptly squandered all the wealth. With nothing left, the younger son ended up working on a farm feeding swine. Realising that even his father's servants had more than he did, the younger son felt remorseful. So he went back home to volunteer to work for his father as a servant.

When the younger son came home, what do you think the father did?

He ran out to meet the son—which is something that a patriarch of that generation would never do. Not only that, the father embraced the son, welcoming him back into the family. Then he killed the big calf and called the whole village to party, celebrating his son's return.

Meanwhile, the elder son came to the father angry. He'd always faithfully served his father—and never even received a small goat for a party! The elder son was hurt—feeling he'd been treated unfairly.

The father explained that everything he had *already* belonged to the elder son. It was right to celebrate, said the father, because the younger son (who the father thought was dead) was actually alive. He was lost but now was found.

Well, then—the elder son came to the party and it was all happy-ever-

---

[26] Luke 15:11-32

after. They celebrated God's amazing blessings, and the elder son was wonderfully reconciled with his younger brother.

Hold on. Wait a minute. That last bit doesn't sound familiar, does it?

That's because it's not. I changed it.

The real story ends with the father speaking to the elder son, explaining that it's right to celebrate. And that's it. Nothing else. On many levels, the story is unresolved.

We never find out what happened.

We don't know if the brother went to the youngest son's party or not. We don't know if the elder son reconciled with the younger son... or whether the elder son turned around and left in anger. And we don't know how the whole event impacted the elder son's relationship with his father.

So what really happened?

There's no satisfactory, Hollywood ending. No happy Christian resolution to the story.

It's unresolved. Like so many of our own stories today.

Unresolved Stories

Remember my friend, Tanya, who I mentioned in a previous chapter? Myalgic Encephalomyelitis is a neurological and autoimmune condition that leaves her unable to live life in the way that most of us do. She's exhausted much of the time, needing to rest often.

It's a major mission for her to go out of the house. Her life is compounded by the British National Health Service (NHS) not recognising her condition. As Tanya once said, "Every single attempt to get the NHS to treat me feels like a battle." Oh, some doctors believe in her condition and accept it. But then they're unable to prescribe medication because more medics don't believe in the condition. She's fighting an ongoing battle, trapped in an endless cycle of specialists and doctors, attempting to get proper treatment.

Tanya's situation is, purely and simply, unresolved.

Even though Tanya is a Christian, there's no happy-ever-after story here. It's not all, "Let's pray and get healed; you'll get the appointments that you need and you'll get the medication formula that works." In the end, because she still has the condition, the result is that she feels even more tired.

It's living proof that things don't always work out okay.

The world is full of unresolved stories. Broken lives. People who've made mistakes. The person not healed. The relative dying from cancer or with a condition and staying on medication. Or the abusive husband who doesn't leave . . . or who comes back.

God doesn't always resolve issues, no matter how much we want Him to. I don't know why, but He doesn't.

We all know it. Yet Christians can pretend that the world is perfect, like God always solves our problems, as if every story has the happy ending and we don't need to worry. The attitude of naïveté—that life is all good in the Christian bubble, that suffering is outside of me, that life is all happy ending stories—is cheap grace.

With cheap grace, you and I might not have to confront the realities of pain in our own lives or the lives of others. We may not have to confront the suffering of the world that we live in or the uncomfortable side of discipleship and personal growth.

In cheap grace, you and I might try to avoid the edge of grace. It can be very tempting. If we choose to avoid the edge of grace, we don't have to ask the difficult question many of us want to ask, but don't:

Where are you, God?

In order to have an authentic church, to have a culture that confronts problems rather than ignores them, and to become true disciples of Jesus Christ, we have to be aware of and embrace the cost of grace.

Grace in Action

With sober eyes, we have to take a long, hard look at the cost of grace.

We have to be honest with our addictions, bad habits, and hurts. We have to confront the things we're ashamed of—secrets and all. Then we must be willing to pay the cost of grace, which is to change our lives and live differently in spite of pain and error. And keep moving forward.

We must open our eyes to the world that we live in—and take action. To address the hurt. To be there for those without answers.

Some Christians might argue, wasn't the idea of the cross that we don't have to pay the cost? Didn't the cross take care of the consequences of our mistakes? Shouldn't we just be celebrating the resurrection and new life through Christ without worrying the cost?

That's the view of many Christians. They argue that Jesus has taken care of everything, so all we have to do is celebrate and embrace the victory. Forget the cost.

But choosing to be a disciple of Jesus is not pain-free.

Let's be clear: I'm not talking about salvation itself. Salvation by grace means saying yes to Jesus, and that "yes" reconciles us with Him. We're brought together in a right relationship with God. That's *saying yes* to the forgiveness that we already have in Christ.

Saying yes to forgiveness opens the door to eternal life, which is for all of us, wherever we are. Grace opens us up to receive salvation in the midst of our mess, in the moment that we are most exposed, and to know we are infinitely loved.

We can stay there, if we like. We can accept Jesus into our lives and know the full love and blessing of God in salvation.

Sometimes, even, staying in the place that feels good is precisely what we need. It's a space for receiving grace, celebrating it in the comfort zone. And it's good.

As long as we don't stay there.

Moving Beyond the Saving Grace to Active Grace

Eventually, if we're serious about the way of Jesus, we all come to a point where we need to move forward. That moving forward is to become *disciples*—not just believers. Being a disciple is knowing the price, knowing there are tough decisions, and fully turning over our lives to learning at His feet. It can be a high price.

And the price is different for us all.

For some, the price of costly grace is confronting a hurt in our past that we've buried or tried to numb with habits or behaviours. For others, it may be a relationship to change. It might even mean giving up a job.

You may have heard it said before: To find out what's really important to a person, the only thing you need to do is check his or her bank statement. It's there, where the money resides, where we discover our real priorities—where we give most of our resources.

What's really important to us?

In order to show grace in action, we may need to re-assess our priorities in life. If we're willing to pay costly grace rather than cheap grace, we get more. You get what you pay for.

What cost are you willing to pay, to be who God wants you to be?

Do you and I sit in our comfort zones, not growing, not going deeper with God? Or do we make our faith the actions of grace in a world of fear?

Because real Grace disrupts our lives. And it's good. Consider Grace's disruption. Embrace it.
Let it transform.

James Prescott

Chapter 10: Renew
Powerful Grace and Change

"Grace transforms our failings full of dread
into abundant, endless comfort.
Our failings full of shame
into a noble, glorious rising.
Our dying full of sorrow
into holy, blissful life."
Julian Of Norwich, *Revelations of Divine Love*[27]

We are called to live a transformed life.

A transformed life is a new life, orientated around a new set of values.
Jesus Christ calls us to live according to a new agenda and a new economy.
He wants us to be transformed by His grace into the people He created us
to be.

Not to live by the story our culture tells us.

Culture tells us that life is about us—our needs, our wants, and our
happiness. Culture says we must have more, in order to have a happy life.
Culture says that the *right relationship, right money, right job, right holiday,* and
right possessions will make it all better.

And culture says we only get these good things by earning them.

Grace isn't like that.

Grace is not about getting what we deserve. It's not about "living the right
kind of life," and then you get all that you need. As we said before, grace
is costly. And grace's cost is about a change. Risk. Sacrifice.

---

[27] *Revelations of Divine Love* (2011), The Order of Julian of Norwich, Paraclete
Press: Brewster.

Practically Speaking

There are many places where grace's cost may show up in our lives. Some may argue that not having sex outside of marriage is a sacrifice. I've spoken to non-Christians who, whilst they respect my beliefs totally, have no idea how saving sex is maintained.

But I choose this way gladly, because I know that it's the best way to live.

Do I have days where I wish I could have sex outside of marriage? Yes, of course I do. But I never give in to that temptation, because I've seen a life that's better. Because I'm convinced the way of Jesus is the best way to be a human being, and that the way of purity before marriage is better than any other alternative. It's actually not a burden. It's actually quite liberating.

But overall, because of culture, there are many places where following Jesus isn't easy. It's not simple. It costs us.

Some don't want to make too many sacrifices to follow Jesus. They just want the blessing—the forgiveness, healing, and restoration. None of these are truly free. Just ask Jesus.

He'll show you His hands, His feet and His side.

A Story

I would like to tell a story about someone I know. I think it took a lot of guts for this person to share her story with me because she really messed up. To admit faults is hard to do, so I admire her.

Hers is a great story of grace and transformation. The story doesn't start out well, though.

Several years ago, this woman—we'll call her Mary—was in a difficult place all over her life. Mary just didn't see it. At work, Mary had just moved into a new department. Part of her job was analyzing data and writing reports…nothing too glamorous. What she was doing certainly wasn't what she had felt called to do, in the overall scheme of her life. Mary confided in me that she felt a calling to work in Christian leadership.

In her mind, the job Mary was in was just a temporary job, until she found her "real" calling.

Mary told me that she was under-performing, and she didn't care about doing her best in the situation she was in. Because she didn't want to be in the job in the first place, she completely slacked off.

Mary confided to me that she lived in a fantasyland, where (in her mind) doors were going to magically open and suddenly, all of her dreams of the perfect life would fall into her lap. Success. Popularity. Status. A great husband and family. She would wake up one day, and it would all be there.

Real life and her fantasy life were in direct conflict.

The biggest part of her conflict was that she enjoyed her life, there in the fantasy. Imagining that her life was going to be wonderful very soon was easier than engaging with real life. In truth, in every area of her real life, she didn't like herself, let alone love herself.

During this time, she says she became lazy and didn't take care of herself (hard to believe now, seeing the person she is today). It wasn't intentional. She wasn't thinking deeply at the time.

She realizes now that she had an internal belief that good things don't happen to her. There was no point in doing the work to become successful because, subconsciously, she thought she'd never get there.

Soon people began to notice her lack of self-care. She didn't keep up on her clothes or keep herself tidy. She didn't fix her hair. She gained weight. I guess you could say she let herself go.

Fortunately for Mary, she had a manager who was a top guy. He didn't just care about getting the job done well. The manager actually cared about the people he worked with, encouraging and supporting them, even if it meant saying something difficult.

Mary was about to experience that first hand.

She recounts their meeting in the manager's private office:
"He talked about the problems with my work and how under-performing

I was. He said I needed to shape up and do the job I was hired for, or I could go under disciplinary procedures and potentially lose the job. I was shocked when he said that there was no excuse, that it had to be sorted out right now or I'd lose my job.

And then he got personal. He told me that he thought I needed to not wear the same outfit every day, and that I needed to at least take care of my hair as a way of showing value for myself. He actually told me that I had an odour problem. I could tell by his demeanour that he wasn't trying to be mean. And he wasn't trying to step over a personal line. He really cared.

But the manager's words cut like a sharp knife. It was like someone had taken a Samurai sword to my spirit and pierced my soul. It was painful. Very painful. Overwhelming, in fact. Because I knew it was true. I knew I wasn't being professional. I knew I was slacking off, and I knew I was being lazy and not taking care of myself."

It's awfully brave to admit this all, isn't it?

And the story doesn't end there. Mary's manager had more to say.

According to Mary, he let her know that he believed in her, he supported her, and he wanted to help her. He would back Mary up in any action she wanted to take, including holding her accountable to make her changes. The manager's final words were that he believed Mary could genuinely turn the situation around, working together.

He showed grace. He really cared.

At this point, Mary was overwhelmed. She had completely and utterly let down someone whom she had respected and liked. She had betrayed the manager's faith in her. In fact, her exact words to me were, "I'd been selfish, lazy, and unprofessional. And we both knew it."

Mary's soul was stripped bare with the exposure to the truth. But the person who exposed it also comforted her by believing in her and supporting her.

That kind of honesty is transforming.

James Prescott

In Mary's dark moment, she felt deep emotional pain, but she also felt a sense of being valued, loved, and accepted.

Even in telling me this story, Mary broke down in tears. She said she apologised to her manager with pretty much every known expression of apology, and thanked him for being honest. She promised to make the necessary changes and turn the situation around.

And she did.

The Mary today is completely transformed from the Mary back then.

The point is that Mary changed her life. She took care of her self. She came to work with a different attitude. And over time, after confronting the difficult truth, there was a transformation.

Mary's manager treated her with grace. Mary received the difficult news through the grace that went along with it—then responded by taking action.

After a time, Mary told me that she started getting really good feedback from the other managers. Her work was even used as a benchmark for office employees. And she became a fully integrated part of that work team.

She went from one of the least-performing members of the team to one of the best.

What happened here?

Transformation Rooted in Value

She received the truth in grace by someone who loved her and cared for her. She took action on it. She began to value herself. And she was transformed.

If we don't value ourselves, it's difficult to change. And if we can't accept that we're accepted as we are by God—if we think we're condemned—then we have no motivation for change.

Let me say it another way.

If we can't believe that we are valuable, loveable, and accepted by God just as we are, then we can't grow and move forward because we are trying to prove ourselves all the time. And we'll never be enough.

When we don't like ourselves, we try to make ourselves worthy by what we do. We feel a gap inside, and we want to fill it. We strive. We try to get our worth by others' affirmations. But if we're building our life around getting accolades, then you and I are going to be disappointed.

We have to accept ourselves, first. And if God accepts us as we are, then shouldn't we accept ourselves, as well?

You are enough.

Even with your imperfections.
Even with what you don't like about yourself.
Even with your failures.

Grace says you're already enough.

Some may say, if we're enough then why change? We are *enough* because we're created and loved by God—a God who is also a just God. As sinners (people who "screw up"), in His justice, we deserve God's wrath but are shown God's grace. Jesus' sacrifice on the cross satisfies the penalty for sin—death—and our call is to respond in faith.

Therefore, true grace compels us to change.

When we receive and know the true depths of grace, there is no way we can refuse change. It is the only possible response.

Receiving grace and forgiveness is humbling. To know God forgives me for my mistakes, that I am released from the past and free to live a new life—and am loved and accepted, even in the midst of my deepest struggles—can be overwhelming.
That's grace. True grace demands a healthy response that is one of its costliest dimensions.

It's not enough merely to confront our mistakes and own up to them. It's not enough to get the amazing feeling of receiving forgiveness. We must choose to live differently—to truly let the past be past and live a new story, a better story.

If we don't, then it's questionable whether we've received grace at all. If we admit our mistakes and receive forgiveness, but then don't commit to change, we are simply going to make the same mistakes again. We might even take steps backwards.

Grace challenges us to "sin no more"—to live differently. To make an active change to our attitudes, to our lifestyle, and to the life we were living before.

It calls us into a new tomorrow.

Is this easy? No. It is not.

Plan to Fail, Plan to Succeed

Inevitably, we will make mistakes. We will stumble and fall. So instead of being afraid of slipping up, let's you and I embrace the truth: We are going to make errors. No matter what life we choose to live, mistakes will be part of it.

So let's make mistakes as part of our transformation, instead of making mistakes that lead us on a downward spiral into darkness. Even two steps forward and one step back is one step forward.

Choosing to live by grace isn't an easy choice. It's tough. It won't be pain free. But God knows we aren't perfect. He doesn't expect us to get it right straightaway.

It's a process.

Grace says we can trust God—because even if we do fall down, we are still loved, accepted, and forgiven.

God never gives up on us.

We don't need to fear change. We can confidently commit to transformation, knowing that if and when we do fall down, His hand is there, ready to pick us up. And then, we are not afraid to step out again. We get up, dust ourselves down, and go and sin no more.

Pots and Making Mistakes

There was an experiment a few years ago with pot makers.[28] The people in charge divided a class into two groups. One group was instructed to try and make as many pots as possible; the other group was instructed to make one great work of art—only one piece, but of the best quality possible.

The experiment showed that the group who made lots of pots produced the better quality work. The researchers concluded the reason the pots were a better quality was that the pot-makers had learned from their mistakes.

On the other hand, the people who tried to make one pot to perfection made mistakes, but didn't learn from them. On top of that, the pot-makers became so caught up in the theory and ideas of *what made a great pot* that it actually hindered their ability to create a great work.

If we don't learn from our mistakes, we aren't going to grow.

Instead, we're going to keep trying to live a perfect life—one that we think we have to live—and our life won't be as beautiful as it is designed to be. This is about perfectionism, isn't it? It's about aiming so high that we give up before we begin. It's about giving up the first time that we fail.

When we acknowledge our mistakes, accepting ourselves—when we allow grace in the door and then keep on trying, being bold and willing to make

mistakes, learning from them—then we can become the beautiful works of art God created us to be.

We have to give ourselves the freedom to fail.

---

[28] Rob Bell, *Drops Like Stars*, New York: Harper Collins, pp. 106-108.

James Prescott

Chapter 11: Hope
Transforming Grace

"There they are. There *we* are—
the multitude who so wanted to be faithful, who at times got defeated,
soiled by life, and bested by trials,
wearing the bloodied garments of life's tribulations,
but through it all clung to faith."
Brennan Manning[29]

Pain leads us to a grace where you and I can discover hope.

In hope, you and I realise that nothing—no mistake, no addiction, no bad decision, no illness, and not even death itself—is the end. There's a future. And it's good.

With hope, we leave the past in its place. But we don't forget the past. We simply don't let that pain define our future.

We find ways to move forward, to learn how to forgive those people who were previously unforgivable—no matter how long and arduous a process it may be.

In the upcoming companion book to *Mosaic of Grace* called *Stories of Grace*, the opening chapter is about my own personal pain of when my Mum died. My Mum dying was the worst day of my life, the most painful experience I've ever gone through. Grief, I found, is the most difficult emotion for me to deal with.

Going through healing from my Mum's death wasn't a short process. There's no quick fix for suffering.

Grace isn't an instant solution. Grace is a journey.

Grace picked me up in the midst of the valley of death, and it showed me

---

[29] Brennan Manning, *The Ragamuffin Gospel: Good News for the Bedraggled, Beat-Up, and Burnt Out* (2005), Crown Publishing, Chapter One.

a way forward. Grace showed me a life beyond my darkest day. As I walked the painful path, I discovered transformation and hope.

And that hope goes beyond us.

Grace's Healing Hope

If you choose to hope and choose to look outward, the scars of your pain eventually bring healing to someone else's life.

This is how grace works.

You see, the most amazing joy for me is being able to use my own scars to bring some form of healing to the lives of others. Helping others has brought new depths of healing for my own pain. What I went through no longer feels like a burden but a privilege. It's no longer a weight on my shoulders; the past pain is an opportunity to serve others.

Through grace, my suffering has been transformed to someone else's hope. It's one of the biggest honours of my life.

This is how the universe works. This is how it's meant to be: Grace meeting us in the death of Friday, leading us to the resurrection of Sunday, and then being poured out into someone else's life.

Grace and hope are intertwined.

Suffering and Human Kintsugi

The season of grief, after the loss of my Mum, may be over. But this doesn't mean I'm done suffering. During the first draft of this book, I dealt with some anxiety, financial worries, and pain from my past that kept coming up and affecting me. We all have seasons in life where we suffer, in many different ways.

In the imperfect world we live in, it's the same for us all. No one can avoid suffering. And if we have already suffered, we will suffer again.

Hope means that no matter how low we may feel, how irreparable our life might appear, or how angry we get with our Creator (or anyone else, for that matter) in the midst of the challenges of life—the one thing we don't have to be in this life is alone.

It's a truth: When we're in the midst of suffering, we often want nothing to do with God.

Why would we?

When we suffer, no matter what we believe about God, we're going to be upset. We're going to get angry, and we're going to ask why.

Suffering forces us to see the world differently. Pain alters our perceptions. After what happens in the pain, we have to get to a new view of God. Suffering sifts us out: we can't go back, and we can't undo what has happened.

We have no choice but to move forward into a different reality.

When in pain, it's easier for us to be controlled by anger. We can think God is picking on us, or we may look for something we've done wrong "to deserve this punishment."

But God is none of these things.

God is in the midst of our suffering. He loves us, and He suffers with us. He is a loving Father who had to watch His own Son unjustly suffer torture, humiliation, and execution—and who knows the full depths of our despair.

Jesus has been through the horror of it all, and he has the scars to prove it. When we are in the depths of suffering, Jesus' ability to know us and love us *in the pain* is what we have to hold on to.

We might still question God; we might still be angry with Him. But when we view God through grace, then there is less chance we'll abandon Him because we know the truth. If by the edge of our fingernails, we can manage to hold on to the truth even in the darkest depths of the shadows, we begin to find hope.

We see the promise in tomorrow.

As the man who took the pieces of Ashikaga Yoshimasa's broken bowls and turned the pieces into beautiful works of Kintsugi said, "Now, [the bowls are] even better than when you bought them."[30] The art of Kintsugi—the art of a golden joinery—rejoices in brokenness.

This is profound, for you and for me.

God's Kintsugi

When a Kintsugi joiner sees a shattered, broken bowl, he or she does not see an end like others would.

The joiner sees an opportunity.
A chance for a new beginning.

And what is created as a result has greater value than it ever had before. Something more beautiful than anyone else had imagined.

This is what happens when we experience grace.

Understand this. Let it sink in.

Grace breaks us apart but puts us back together more beautifully than we have been before.

When we are put back together by God's hands, we are more aware of our true value than ever before.

No matter how broken our lives, God picks up the pieces and puts them back together to make something more precious and more beautiful than we could ever have imagined.

A Kintsugi of Grace

Through our re-made lives, through grace, there is hope. Resurrection. The chance of a new tomorrow. For all of us.
There was a time in my life that I've already alluded to, when I reached a

---

[30] https://dicklehman.wordpress.com/2013/04/18/kintsugi-gold-repair-of-ceramic-faults-2/, accessed December 13, 2016.

really low point in my faith. The ghosts of my past came back to haunt me, and I was getting low, angry, and frustrated. I doubted God. I questioned if He even existed. My past overwhelmed me, and my insecurities began to control me. What began as healthy questioning had, in hindsight, descended into despair.

God had continually, for years, been telling me the same thing: *You think you're worthless, but I say you're worth everything.*

It can be hard to grasp. But it's the truth.

Even in times where I've believed that I'm worth everything to God, I've still had my rants at God. (Haven't you?) At that time, when something even remotely bad happened, I exploded in an angry rage. The hurt from my past was still present, influencing my thinking and feelings.

And every time I ranted, I said the same lines to God: *Why are you doing this to me? You're just teasing me aren't you? You don't love me, you just pretend to.*

Then one day, during one of these rants, I said without thinking, *I hate you.*

That claim led me to more ranting at God. I even thought I was okay. But something deeper was happening. Growing in God brought out past pains, insecure thoughts, and issues that I had to face. And they weren't letting go of me.

I soon realised that I had to let go of them.

One Sunday in church, the pastor preached about how God isn't always nice to us. He doesn't always say what we want to hear. The truth hit me, and I distinctly heard that inner voice of God saying, *enough is enough. No more of these rants. No more false accusations. It needs to stop.*

When are you going to believe that you are worth everything to me?

I asked someone to pray for me. The person praying for me said that, while praying, she had a picture in her mind of a lost lamb. And the idea that came to her was that God had left the other 99 lambs and gone to search for this one lamb.

I was the lamb. I had been lost, and God had left the 99 and come to find me.[31]

And I belonged to Him.

For someone who had rarely, if ever, felt like he belonged, this word picture—and its truth—was overwhelming. I *had* been lost. God *had* come and found me. He would do it again. And keep on doing it, if He had to.

I had been in the pit of despair and had been rescued. I am incredibly valuable.

And so are you.

My life didn't suddenly become all okay that day. I'm like everyone else on this planet. I have insecurities. I have pain.

We all do.

But now, when I'm in the midst of the lost feelings, when I'm stripped naked and exposed for the world to see, I reach out with what little faith I have and grab hold of a hand. It's a bloody hand, but a strong one. And He doesn't let go of me. He lifts me up and brings me home.

This is the hand of someone who doesn't suddenly make it all okay but meets me in the midst of my pain. A man who takes me as I am: hurt, bruised, bitter, and sometimes distant—and loves me. Who exposes the truth of who I am, and challenges me to work with Him in a process of healing and transformation.

The Hand of grace. Reaching out to us. Embracing us *exactly as we are*. And loving us way too much to let us stay where we are right now.

In the world where a relative gets incurable cancer.
Where we are raped or abused by someone we trusted.
Where someone we love dies suddenly and unexpectedly.

---

[31] "Suppose one of you has a hundred *sheep* and loses one of them. Doesn't he leave the ninety-nine in the open country and go after the lost *sheep* until he finds it?" Luke 15:4, New International Version, the Bible.

Where disappointments come and surround us.

Circumstances can lead us to becoming cynical, negative, and depressed. Raw challenges have the potential to ultimately lead us to a place where we give up on hope. A place where we give up on God.

And give up on grace.

We may miss grace out of cynicism. Or we may miss grace because we don't want to face the truth of who we are. We might not want to be stripped bare, so that we can begin the process of transformation. Or maybe we'd rather like to receive the, *I do not condemn you,* part of Jesus— but conveniently ignore the *go and sin no more* part.

The simple truth is that grace is found within moments of pain, suffering, and violence. When we have nothing left to give, when the world has deserted us, and when all hope appears to be gone, grace remains.

And through grace, we discover hope.

Real Hope in Jesus Christ

Jesus isn't some distant person who knows nothing about suffering. He doesn't come with a smiley fix-it-all face. He's not someone disconnected from the darkest depths of despair

Oh, no.

This man is familiar with loneliness, torture, injustice, grief, humiliation, abuse, and abandonment.

The hand of grace is the hand of a Man who, though totally innocent, was convicted and sentenced to death. He was beaten, spat upon, pushed to the ground and tortured within an inch of his life. He was covered in blood, carried a piece of wood heavier than him for a long distance, and then, stripped completely naked, was nailed to it for the whole world to see. Insulted, made fun of, spat upon, abandoned by all but his Mother and a couple of friends.

He was a Man who died bloody, who died violently, and who endured great physical, emotional, and spiritual torture. It's the risen hand of this

Man that reaches us when we're in the gutter, and He lifts us out of the hopelessness with a hand that knows pain.

He doesn't promise that life will suddenly be okay. The scars remain, and the pain may not be ended. And there may be more pain to come. But this Man gives us a gift of Hope in Him. We can allow ourselves to be loved in the midst of suffering by One who has literally been there.

Jesus' open hand is always there, even when we don't feel it. He waits for us to grasp hold with what might be the last energy we have, and receive the gift His grace gives.

With the hope His grace brings, we become positively overwhelmed by grace. Forever. In facing up to the truth of our lives, we allow ourselves to be transformed, loved, and healed. And, eventually, in the process of His grace pouring over us, we discover true, intimate, deep joy.

Then we know: Hope and grace are not myths, but exist in actual fact.

Jesus is His name.

Jesus wants to take the shattered glass of our broken lives and put it back together. He wants to make something new and even more precious from the broken glass that seemed destroyed and irreparable. God wants to turn the broken glass of our lives into a beautiful mosaic for the world to see.

Grace is Action

Grace is forward movement. When we are at our end, Grace invites us to grab hold of His hand with all we have left and commit to a new way of life, one staggering step at a time. Even if it's only by the edges of our fingertips, grace leads us to hope.

Grace is disruption. When the worst has happened, Grace says the worst thing isn't the end. In positive disruption, grace challenges us to commit to ongoing transformation.

Grace is more than just an emotional feeling or a celebration. It becomes an intimate encounter with the divine, a moment of transformation and restoration. We experience joy deeper than we could ever know.

Grace is a miracle. It's foreign to anything we encounter in our world. It's beyond anything we can understand or know.

Grace Extending

Through our transformation, the world too, begins to experience grace.

Because as we dare to step out and confront our own brokenness and suffering, healing and restoration can begin in our relationships. And when we dare to step out and confront the brokenness and suffering of the world, healing and restoration can begin around us.

Extending grace means that broken lives are put back together—our lives and others' lives. When we extend grace, the kingdom becomes a bit more real, piece-by-piece.

We know that we'll walk in shadowy places again. But whatever happens, we have Hope to cling to, with a confidence that no matter how dark the circumstance, no matter how painful life becomes, we can find our way with Grace.

James Prescott

Chapter 12: How
Living Out Grace

_____

"When I look at the Cross of Christ,
what I see up there is all my s**t—and everybody else's.
So I ask myself a question a lot of people have asked:
Who is this man?"
Bono[32]

We've talked a lot in this book about the theory of grace: its meaning, how it impacts our view of God, the contrast between law and grace, what costly grace is, how grace has an edge, and how grace leads us through to transformation and hope.

But where do we go from here?

I mean, it's great to discuss these issues. But real impact can only come with living grace out, in practice.

Where is grace at work right now?

In 1932, there was a magazine spread in *Homes and Gardens*[33] about a prominent politician of the day. The politician's family was friendly, and they had great art in their house. He was a strict vegetarian, was good with children, and played Mozart on their piano. Generally, a nice and friendly person, eh?

Except the politician's name was Adolf Hitler.

You see, it's important not to judge others on what they say, or even how they are with us, one-on-one. We all know: The totality of our being doesn't lie in what we *say* we believe. It's in what we *do*.
Hitler might have been friendly and polite on a one-to-one basis, but it

_____

[32] https://junglenotes.wordpress.com/tag/bono/, accessed December, 2016.

[33] https://www.theguardian.com/world/2003/nov/03/secondworldwar.blogging, accessed December 13, 2016.

wasn't the totality of who he was. He was an evil monster, responsible for countless deaths in World War II and the Holocaust. We judge Hitler's actions, and rightly so.

In the same way, people won't judge us on what we say or how we are, one-to-one. What we truly believe, who we truly are, will always be best demonstrated by our actions in the long run. It's what we do that defines us.

If we say we believe in grace, yet we don't live through the lens of grace, then are we really who we say we are? If we aren't advocates and examples of grace, allowing our lives to be transformed and showing grace to others, then are we who we say we are?

If we're to truly become a people of grace, transforming this world by grace in us, then we have to expose ourselves to the edge of grace and, with courage, allow God permission to expose the areas of our lives needing transforming, healing, and restoration. And then we can—and must—choose to live differently. So that we, like works of Kintsugi, are restored to a beautiful mosaic.

I can't say it enough. Exposure can be painful. Uncomfortable. Disruptive. And exposure can take time. But once we go through the pain, we experience healing, restoration, and ultimately, transformation.

Transformation is also a choice that we keep making. It's a choice to be honest. Honest with ourselves and with those we know about our weaknesses and flaws.

The cycle of honesty, exposure, and transformation is the act of growing in grace.

Today's Culture

Today's culture goes against the cycle of grace.

Our culture misses what is most important, and so many of us are obsessed and consumed with the things in life that simply don't matter.

So many have settled for a life where the biggest fun is getting drunk and having sex. For so many, life is about working a job you don't really love but pays the bills. So many are caught in spending money and, ultimately, the spending hides the deep truth of being unsatisfied, unfulfilled, and feeling like there's no hope of escaping the every-day story.

The world judges us by how much money we have or our looks. The irony is that most people—despite what we might think—don't actually look like supermodels or film stars and aren't millionaires. Even more importantly, in the end, the people who *do* have money, status, or a wild lifestyle realize that all those things don't solve their problems. Ultimately, the things of the world make our inner problems even bigger.

We tend to believe the lie that there is a hole in us that can magically be filled by whatever it is we worship: money, sex, status, success, or religion. In truth, there is no hole. And we don't need anything to complete us or make us whole.

We don't "lack." We already have infinite value and worth. We are already infinitely loved and accepted *as we are*. We've messed up. All of us. And God's forgiveness is waiting for us. If there is a need, it is the need for us to accept the grace that has already been extended.

Grace is God's gift to us.

The only choice we have to make is whether to accept grace or not. Whatever we choose, there are consequences either way. But it's our choice. It is our action to take. Grace demands action.

Showing Grace to Others

God wholly sees those around us and loves and accepts them anyway. Seeing and understanding God's perspective changes our perspective.

God's ability to give grace is our example.

Even when our personal mess is exposed and stripped bare for the world, we can show grace to others. Like receiving grace, showing grace is a choice. It's often an uncomfortable, difficult choice, and it's a decision we'll keep on making, again and again.
It's a choice to give by grace. Repeatedly.

It's counter-cultural.

Forgiving the parent who abused us.
Forgiving the friend who betrayed us.
Forgiving the partner who cheated on us.

This grace is costly.

There's still a part of me wanting revenge on the bullies from my childhood. But whenever the feeling of revenge rises up, I have to choose to say *no*. I have to choose not to hold a grudge, to forgive them. I have to choose to love, instead. The pain from my past can't do any more damage to me than it has already done. Extending grace allows me to see others as God sees them.

Grace allows me to realize how God sees me. And you. We are broken people who have made mistakes but are still infinitely loved, with infinite value.

Living Imperfectly

Are we going to miss the mark and fall short? Of course we are.

We aren't perfect, and forgiveness towards those who have wronged us—towards those who have inflicted great pain—is one of the most difficult things that we can ever do.

It's better to live in forgiveness than to carry around anger, hatred, and bitterness. Living in grace-filled forgiveness is better than living a life fuelled by rage. Living in grace is better than treating others poorly because they hurt you.

The truth is, you are capable of living in grace. We all are.

The World Needs Grace

What about the world we live in?

Our world is far from perfect. There are a lot of people—both Christians and non-Christians—who, when it comes to grace, are cynical.

And rightly so.

The real power of grace comes in exposing truth. So let's look at the truth about the world in which we live.

In 2016, the Global Slavery index stated there are approximately 45.8 million people in slavery in 167 different countries (www.globalslaveryindex.org/findings). According the US State Department, between 600,000-800,000 people are trafficked across international boundaries each year—70 per cent of them female.[34] And nearly 18,000 of them are trafficked into the US.[35] Trafficking is the world's third largest criminal industry—behind arms trafficking and illegal drugs. It generates approximately $32 billion each year.[36]

And then there's the water crisis. Also as of 2016, according to The World Health Organization, 663 million people (1 in 10) lack access to safe water, and 2.4 billion people (1 in 3) lack access to a toilet. Indeed, more people have access to a mobile phone than a toilet.[37]

In the US alone, there are 15 million in poverty—yes, in the United States—and nearly 3 billion people (almost half the world's population)

---

[34] https://www.dosomething.org/us/facts/11-facts-about-human-trafficking, accessed August 1, 2016.

[35] Ibid.

[36] Ibid.

[37] http://water.org/water-crisis/water-sanitation-facts/ and http://www.who.int/water_sanitation_health/monitoring/jmp-2015-update/en/, accessed September 5, 2016.

live on $2.50 a day.[38]

Right on my doorstep in the UK, the number of people helped by Foodbanks (a Christian led organisation providing three days' worth of food to those with no way of feeding themselves financially) has grown from approximately 25,000 in 2008-2009, to over 1.1 million in 2015-2016.[39]

And this isn't taking into account the rise of terrorism around the world, the emerging refugee crisis, and the huge increase in gun crime.

So anyone of faith who goes around saying everything is fine—that there are no problems and we're all happy as long as our own lives are okay—is lying. Any Christian who says, *if you believe rightly, suddenly everything will take care of itself*—is lying.

Many churches act like the above problems don't exist. In fact, western consumer culture encourages us to act like they don't exist. We're encouraged to simply give to charity and then we've "done our bit" and can go on like the problems don't exist. And whilst giving to charity is a good thing, if everyone only gave to charity, would anything get done? Of course, not.

These problems demand action.

I'm not here to guilt anyone into anything. I'm not interested in that. But if we want to live in a world of grace, we can't ignore the uncomfortable truth about the world we live in.

There are organisations heeding grace's call to action.

International Justice Mission (IMJwww.ijm.org) is an organisation founded and led by Gary Haugen. It works to combat human trafficking, including the commercial sexual exploitation of children, forced labour

---

[38] The Institute for Research on Poverty, http://www.irp.wisc.edu/faqs/faq3.htm, accessed September 5, 2016.

[39] https://www.trusselltrust.org/news-and-blog/latest-stats/, accessed September 5, 2016.

slavery, illegal detention, police brutality and illegal land seizure—regardless of faith background. And it's making a difference.

The organisation's work in Cebu, Philippines, was shown to have reduced the number of minors in the sex trade by 79 percent.[40] Over 200 minors were rescued, over 700 law enforcement officials were trained, and over 100 traffickers were charged.[41] In 2011, IJM worked with local authorities to free over 2500 bonded labourers in the Indian states of Tamil Nadu and Andra Pradesh, since 2001.[42]

Slavery is a problem in my home country as well.

In the UK, there is a small but growing organisation called Hope for Justice. Hope for Justice (www.hopeforjustice.co.uk) is a non-governmental anti-human trafficking organisation working to uncover and abolish modern-day slavery. They gather intelligence and assist in the process of removing victims from exploitation. In 2014, they rescued 142 victims of human trafficking in the UK.[43]

This is grace in action.

This is a Christian organisation confronting the truth of the world we live in—and taking action to change it.

With the water crisis, you only have to look at Charity: Water[44] to see how faith can impact our world. The fact that the organisation exists at all is a story of grace. It's founder, Scott Harrison, was a big promoter in New

---

[40] https://www.ijm.org/where-we-work/philippines, accessed September 5, 2016.

[41] Ibid.

[42] https://www.ijm.org/where-we-work/india, accessed September 5, 2016.

[43] http://www.bbc.co.uk/news/uk-england-manchester-25630283 and http://hopeforjustice.org/united-kingdom/, accessed September 5, 2016.

[44] Rob Bell, RobCast Episode 29 and "Drop Like Stars" live tour film, and http://www.charitywater.org/about/scotts_story.php, accessed September 5, 2016.

York, very successful, knowing all the right people and making a lot of money.

But Harrison began to find the life he was living distasteful. He saw what his life had become (parties, drinking, sex) and found that he'd lost purpose and meaning. He realised he was spiritually dead and needed radical change.

Despite not knowing anything about photography, he volunteered as a photographer on a Mercy Ship—a hospital ship travelling to needy parts of the world, providing medical services.

The trip profoundly impacted Harrison's life. Seeing people living on 325 dollars a year—an amount that he used to blow in one night on a single bottle of spirits—put faces on the stories of poverty and inequality. Then Harrison noticed that 80 percent of the disease he encountered was caused almost directly by a lack of clean drinking water—causing more death than war.[45]

He knew he had to do something.

Using the contacts from his time as a promoter, Harrison held paid parties and created window displays in major department stores in New York to raise money. Harrison discovered, through his own experience of grace, his life's calling.

Harrison's own story of grace became one that poured out into the lives of others.

What happened then?

As of January 2016, over $200,000,000 has been raised on 20,056 projects, and 6.3 million people have clean drinking water who didn't have it

---

[45] Rob Bell, RobCast Episode 29 and "Drop Like Stars" live tour film, and http://www.charitywater.org/about/scotts_story.php, accessed September 5, 2016.

before.[46] They raised $33 million in 2006 alone for clean water projects, funding 2,000 new water projects and providing 700,000 more people with clean drinking water.[47] [48] Clearly, the momentum to help others is growing. More and more money is being raised, and more and more people are getting access to clean drinking water.

Grace Impacts Others

Grace confronts our truth and transforms us. And then it overflows.

Like Harrison, we should not be afraid to confront the truth about ourselves and confront the world we live in.

The question remains: How can you serve?

I'm honoured to serve at a local Foodbank. A bunch of churches in my hometown of Sutton have come together to provide three days worth of food for people in my community who are in a crisis situation, for whatever reason. We also now have a befriending scheme and give out basic cutlery, sleeping bags to those sleeping under bridges, basic utensils to open and eat their tinned food, and meal vouchers.

During my three years volunteering with the Foodbank, I've been confronted with the harsh reality of the world we live in. So many uncomfortable truths about poverty in our relatively rich western culture made me confront how much I really have, and how materialistic I can be.

It has exposed me to grace.

Serving others allows us to show grace. Whether it's two hours or two days a month, serving makes a big difference in our communities.

You see, we can all be people of grace. Grace that transforms the world

---

[46] http://www.fastcoexist.com/3055110/these-sensors-raise-the-bar-or-accountability-for-water-charities, accessed September 5, 2016.

[47] www.charitywater.org/projects, accessed September 5, 2016.

[48] http://www.charitywater.org/about/financials.php, accessed September 5, 2016.

by exposing and compelling us to change our own lives—and then, positively change the lives of others. Such change—such *grace*—brings genuine hope into our world.

The transforming power of grace in our lives—and grace in the world at large—intertwines. When grace moves within both individuals and communities, problems are out in the open, and authentic, powerful steps can be taken toward solutions. We simply can't stay as we have been. Change is inevitable. Good change. Action.

God made us as part of the solution to the problems of the world. With grace, we can choose to not ignore the very real problems (as consumerism encourages us to do). True grace then allows us to be honest about the suffering, injustice, and evil in the world…and then…

Grace allows us to take a stand against it.

Grace is God's change agent. Grace is the catalyst for transformation in our lives, the lives of others, and the world at large. And through the process of grace, we discover true hope and real joy. Grace transforms literally everything.

People often talk big about "changing the world." But we don't have to be leaders of big world-changing organisations, pastors, politicians, or the next MLK or Gandhi. Although such people do change the world, in reality, you can make a difference.

Real change comes from each of us doing what we can.

It doesn't even matter if no one ever sees or knows what you do. God sees. And the person it blesses does, too. And that, in its own way, makes you as much a world changer as any major historical figure.

Because you've brought something new into existence. You've given hope to someone who had none.

Always remember the mosaic. Through the broken glass of our lives, God puts us back together to make a beautiful mosaic for the world to see. A mosaic transforming how we view and interact with the world. A mosaic reflecting light onto all those who encounter us. In both small and large ways, changing the world.

May you and I be persons who own the truth of who we are, whatever the circumstances.

May we be the person who goes and sins no more.

May we be persons of forgiveness, no matter what people have done to us or against us.

May we take responsibility for the truth of our lives and challenge others to do the same.

May we learn to love and forgive others, even when we know their messes.

May we know the truth of how much we are loved and accepted right here, right now, as we are.

May we not stand in ignorance of the reality of the world we live in, but instead, in our own however-small ways, confront these realities and live to change them.

And finally, may we take the broken glass of the world we live in and accept Jesus' invitation to help transform it into a beautiful work of divine Kintsugi.

A mosaic of grace.

James Prescott

Rising
A Poem by Joy Lenton

We rise up bold...
shaking off dust and ashes,
for we are the brave and free
kicking away the lies
and deceit of the enemy,
now in tatters at our feet

As we take our place
together...
let us embrace
our stories, who we are,
how far we have come,
renewed, redeemed children
of grace and hope,
no longer at the end,
dangling on bitten rope

We are...
rising, climbing strong
to the glory that awaits us
and enjoying the view,
while we eschew all
that no longer belongs
as part of our lives
or hearts

As one...
being light
being salt
being hope,
bringing encouragement
as truth believers
truth bearers,
weavers of story
strong through struggle,

Mosaic of Grace

tensile with tenderness
love and compassion

As we seek
above all things
to be true
to ourselves,
our calling,
to the future
where hope rests
eternal in all
and nothing else
will ever snarl,
trip us up
or make us fall

MOSAIC OF GRACE

Words & Music by Shelly E. Johnson

Verse 1
Just a pile of broken glass
Pieces of a painful past
Shattered by the storms of life
This is all that's left inside

Chorus
He can take the fallen pieces
And lay them in the perfect place
When His work is finally finished
You will be a mosaic of grace

Verse 2
In your pain, you may not see
The beauty of the masterpiece
But there's a greater work of art
Than what each piece alone imparts

Chorus
He can take the fallen pieces
And lay them in the perfect place
When His work is finally finished
You will be a mosaic of grace

Bridge
Hallelujah! Hallelu
To the God who makes all things new
Hallelujah! Hallelu
Hallelu

Chorus
He will take the fallen pieces
And lay them in the perfect place
When His work is finally finished
You are a mosaic of grace
You are a mosaic of grace

(c) 2009 Shelly E. Johnson Music, Inc.

Song Release
A new recording of "Mosaic of Grace" was released January 27, 2017. Find the song on iTunes.

Music Video Release
The first ever music video for "Mosaic of Grace" was released January 20, 2017. Find it on YouTube here: https://www.youtube.com/watch?v= X91vByenLEk

About Artist Shelly E. Johnson
Worship music is not a career choice, it's a calling, and it's one that Worship Artist Shelly E. Johnson has embraced with joyful surrender. Most well-known for writing the heartfelt ballad "Mosaic of Grace" that speaks to God making beauty out of our brokenness, as well as the powerful worship anthem "Power of the Cross," which has been recorded by Natalie Grant, Steve Green, and is being used in churches worldwide,

Shelly has served as worship leader alongside Beth Moore, Tony Nolan, Andy Stanley, and toured North America with renowned Irish Hymn-writers Keith & Kristyn Getty. In September 2014, Shelly released her label debut worship album "Your Kingdom Come" in partnership with LifeWay Worship and Elevate Entertainment. In January 2016, Shelly released her follow up worship album entitled Measureless, which debuted in the top 50 on iTunes, with the lead-off single "Loved Me First" hitting the #1 spot at Christian Radio the entire month of January. Less than six months later in June 2016, Shelly released her first ever live worship album, "Christ Be Everything (LIVE)," recorded and filmed at 1971 Sounds in Atlanta, Georgia.

As LifeWay Worship's 2012 Songwriter of the Year, Shelly spends her time writing songs for the Church, serving as a worship leader at her home church, and traveling the country striving to build the Kingdom of God through her music. Shelly and her husband Jack were married in May 2005 and currently live in Woodstock, Georgia, along with their baby daughter, Mary Carson. Visit www.shellyejohnson.com to learn more and find Shelly on the web on Twitter (@ShellyEJohnson), Instagram (@ShellyEJohnson), and Facebook (Facebook.com/ShellyEJohnson).

Afterword
Here's to the Broken Ones

Here's to the broken ones.

The ones who've been stripped bare and have seen their dark side exposed.
Those of us who have been through the blackest side of the valley.
Who know grief, pain, and injustice.
Who don't recover from cancer.
Who have felt hopeless in the face of circumstances.
And where God doesn't answer prayers for healing.

Here's to you. Because you are not alone.

There are many of us who have walked the painful path before. We survived. We are still here. Life went on.

Others of us know, having weaknesses exposed while travelling the darkest valley imaginable: it is not the end. Rather, it is the beginning.

We survivors know that what might seem the end of everything isn't the end. Even within the midst of the darkest valley, there is a sliver of light.

Maybe, right now, you're still in the valley. Maybe you know that others have survived, but you feel you won't.

Survivors know the hopelessness you feel, the overwhelming sense that nothing can save us from our circumstances.

There is a day where we discover that death isn't the end. Where it begins to get better. When we realise life does go on, and that maybe the worst thing that could have happened just did. And we are still here.

You see, in time, we understand: The broken glass of our lives has been shaped by grace into a beautiful mosaic.

Every moment of suffering, pain, discomfort, hopelessness, anger, and despair will neither be the end nor will it be in vain. In time, we discover a day where we can be the bringer, as well as the receiver, of two of the most powerful words of love:

"Me, too."

In that moment, no matter how much pain we still feel, we realise there is not one other person who will go through life without being broken.

That in truth, we are *all* the broken ones.

Acknowledgements
Bringers of Grace

So many people play a part in a book coming together. Though many of us writers would secretly like it to be all about us, we all know it is never just about us. And here I want to pay tribute to all those who helped make this book a reality.

I want to especially thank those who allowed me to use their stories. Thank you for giving me the opportunity to share your lives.

To Dog, my best friend: Thank you for allowing your story to be shared, for your words of encouragement and support, and for telling me to start writing books instead of reviewing them. You're the brother I never had. Thanks, mate.

Kizzy: For being an amazing friend, for hearing my darkest cries, bringing so much joy and being the best soul twin ever. You rock.

To Joy Lenton: For first giving me the idea for this book, for your beautiful poetry, amazing wisdom and encouragement, and for being a person of grace and a great friend. You have no idea how important you've been to me and to this book.

I also want to thank my writer friends—the ones who encouraged me when I lost confidence and nearly gave up, and the ones who proofread different versions of this book and made me believe I could write a book in the first place. The Tribe Writers community has been amazing. And my fellow Dude Writers (all six of you), you are just awesome. Thanks for not giving up on me.

To Chris Morris: You're a true brother. Thanks for believing me and for giving me the courage to have my own writing journey.

To Wendy van Eyck: Thanks for writing an amazing foreword and for being such an example of grace to me as a true sister in faith.

To the whole Sutton Vineyard Church community: You are a constant source of strength, encouragement, and wisdom. You're my family, and you continue to nurture, strengthen, and challenge my faith.

To Becky and Neil Dawson: Thank you for your wisdom, your love, prayers and friendship, and for seeing what God was doing in me before I did.

To Dawson home group: For being the most wonderful, loving, and supportive little community I could imagine. I love you all.

To Claire Ashurst: For advice on publishing and being an awesome first-level proofreader.

To Erin Brown (a.k.a. Erin Brown Conroy): For dropping in and changing my life. An amazing writer, my editor, and friend—thanks so much for everything. Editing this book for me and together with me brought a new understanding of the depth and power of writing. I'm really looking forward to working with you more.

To Ali: The best sister in the world and an example of grace in so many ways.

To Dad: For believing in my writing gift from such a young age. No doubt, one of the reasons I'm writing now is because of your confidence in me.

To Mum: The biggest example of grace I've ever known. I know you're smiling up in heaven and still telling me how you told me so. I miss you and love you.

To Scott Forrester: For reminding me what I'm capable of. For believing in me and becoming such a wonderful friend and part of our family.

Finally, to Jesus: Only You know just how much grace you've shown me in my life and how much you will continue to give. Thanks for not letting me settle but for helping me confront the truth in my own life. Thank you for this amazing privilege of being able to write and share your message of grace. Thanks so much for choosing me and for not leaving me. This is your book.

And to everyone else who has played a part in this book: Friends, family, writers, anyone I've not mentioned.

I begin and end with you, the reader. This book was written to have us all understand more clearly the message of grace and apply it to our lives. If these writings have impacted one person, that's awesome. And if you've made it this far, to the very end, I'm assuming this book has impacted you in some positive way. Thank you for buying the book and reading it.

About the Author
James Prescott

James Prescott is a writer and author from Sutton, near London in the UK. He blogs regularly at **JamesPrescott.co.uk** on discovering our true identity, exploring our creativity and spirituality, and living authentically to create truly honest and great work.

James is author of *Dance of the Writer: A Beginner's Guide to Authentic Writing* and *Unlocking Creativity*. James hosts a weekly podcast called "Poema," formerly "James Talks," found on iTunes and Podbean.

If you want to connect with James, follow him on Twitter and Facebook. If you want to contact James directly to share your own stories of grace, give feedback, or just connect, simply e-mail james@jamesprescott.co.uk. He'd love to hear from you.

Links to James...
Find James here on the web:

Twitter -- https://twitter.com/jamesprescott77
Instagram -- https://www.instagram.com/jamesprescott77/
Facebook -- http://www.facebook.com/JamesPrescottWriter
Podcast -- https://itunes.apple.com/us/podcast/james-talks/id1044862627
Blog/Website -- http://www.jamesprescott.co.uk/

Coaching with James...
If you're looking for one-on-one coaching to discover your unique voice, or if you're interested in coaching to explore and discover your true identity and calling through the context of grace, e-mail James at james@jamesprescott.co.uk today.

Free stuff with James...
Feel free to go and get these freebies:
http://www.jamesprescott.co.uk/blog/free-stuff

Printed in Great Britain
by Amazon